THE PATH TO UNCONDITIONAL LOVE

LESSONS IN HEART-CENTERED LIVING
FROM OUR ANIMAL TEACHERS

STEPHANIE STEPHAN

Copyright © 2025 by Stephanie Stephan

The Path to Unconditional Love
Lessons in Heart-Centered Living from Our Animal Teachers

All rights reserved.
No part of this work may be used or reproduced, transmitted, stored, or used in any form or by any means graphic, electronic, or mechanical, including but not limited to photocopying, recording, scanning, digitizing, taping, Web distribution, information networks or information storage and retrieval systems, or in any manner whatsoever without prior written permission from the publisher.

In this world of digital information and rapidly-changing technology, some citations do not provide exact page numbers or credit the original source. We regret any errors, which are a result of the ease with which we consume information.

Without in any way limiting the author's and publisher's exclusive rights under copyright, any use of this publication to train generative artificial intelligence (AI) or Large Language Model (LLM) technologies to generate text is expressly prohibited.

This book is for informational purposes only. By providing the information contained herein the author is not diagnosing, treating, curing, mitigating, or preventing any type of disease or medical condition. Before beginning any type of natural, integrative, or conventional treatment regimen, it is advisable to seek the advice of a licensed healthcare professional.

Cover Design by: Kristina Edstrom

An Imprint for GracePoint Publishing (www.GracePointPublishing.com)

GracePoint Matrix, LLC
624 S. Cascade Ave, Suite 201
Colorado Springs, CO 80903
www.GracePointMatrix.com
Email: Admin@GracePointMatrix.com

SAN # 991-6032

A Library of Congress Control Number has been requested and is pending.

ISBN: (Paperback) 978-1-968891-08-4
eISBN: 978-1-968891-09-1

Books may be purchased for educational, business, or sales promotional use.
For distribution queries contact Sales@IPGbook.com
For non-retail bulk order requests contact Orders@GracePointPublishing.com
Printed in U.S.A

DEDICATION

This book is dedicated to all the animals who courageously coinhabit alongside us in all four directions of the Earth, to the energy of our loving Mother Earth, and to Mother Mary and my beloved grandmother who love me to no end.

Acknowledgments

To my daughter,

Thank you for choosing to come into this life journey with me.

It is our soul contract I thank for catapulting me into spirituality where I found the light within the darkness, where I learned to not just live but thrive.

You have been one of the greatest teachers of unconditional love in my spiritual path.

WORDS OF GRATITUDE

Special thanks to my spiritual journey mentors: You each have played an important part in my quest for enlightenment and for that I am eternally grateful.

Mother Mary:
lettersfrommothermary.blogspot.com/
channeled by Reverend Barbara Beach

Angel Raphael:
www.youtube.com/@theangelraphael1063/featured
channeled by Kelly Kolodney

Sharon Sananda:
www.sharonsananda.com/

Dana Micucci:
www.danamicucci.com/

Journeys with Soul:
www.journeyswithsoul.com/
led by Cameron and Glenn Broughton

Beneficial Sound by Wayne Marto:
beneficialsound.org/

Galatic Ashley
https://galacticashley.com/

TABLE OF CONTENTS

Preface 1

Part 1: When Our Hearts Shatter 9
Crossing the Rainbow Bridge 10
Hummingbirds 16

Part 2: The Heart Is the Key 21
What Are Frequencies? 35
Birds in the Himalayas 40

Part 3: Unconditional Love 45
The Watchman and Bobby 47
How Did I Start My Journey? 50
How Do Animals Respond to Energy? 54
Who Are Humans? 56
My First Rainbow Bridge Experience 57
Red Wing Black Bird Song 59
Senior Dog Missing! 61
Mahana, My Little Friend 62
Luna, My Bearded Dragon 64
Charlene, My Childhood Parrot 65
Dragonflies 66
Spikey's Not Eating 67
Dog with Epilepsy 68
The Not-So-Social Cow 69

Crossing the Rainbow, Multiple Stories 71

Part 4: Practicing Opening Our Hearts 75
Clover and Zen, the Rainbow Cats 76
Self-Love: Where to Begin? 81

Part 5: Exuding Healing Energy: Our Animal Companions Will Be Grateful! 103
Hope, the Childless Horse 103
Molly, Horse Kidnapped in Canada 106
How Can We All Bring More Unconditional Love Frequency into the World of Animals? 111
Deer Crossing the Highway 113
Stop Hunting 115
Honor Animals Daily 115
Educate and Advocate 116
Farm Animal Sanctuaries 117
Charlotte, the Angus Cow 118
Helen, the Blind Bison 120

Part 6: Leading a Heart-Centered Life 123
Stephanie's Manifesto 124
Manual to Happiness 129

Part 7: Bathe Animal Companions with the Frequency of Love 207
My Animal Energy Healing Technique 208
Kitty with Stomach Sensitivity 217

Resources 223

"Animals remind us
what it's like to be innocent;
to show and give love unconditionally;
to live care-free.
Beneath all that there's a spirit,
a soul-connection, that longs to speak to us,
to teach us things and guide us on our life's journey.
Communicating with animals is that bridge,
and it's the real deal.
No smoke and mirrors, no gimmicks,
just the heart and soul
of one living, conscious being
connecting to another."

—Pam Roussell

Used with explicit permission granted by the author.

PREFACE

I always joke with my friends about how we are born without a manual. There have been many times I have wished I had one that would tell me how to navigate through life with a little bit more ease. We learn as we go and we do the best we can, but it comes with a cost: We experience pain. The saddest part of this is if we don't figure it out, we unintentionally—and sometimes quite intentionally—inflict pain on others too. We perpetuate the cycle of hurt.

For our well-being and the well-being of those around us, it is our job to figure out how to be happy. Society does not provide a foundation to cultivate happiness as a discipline, as a lifestyle. Hiding from pain does not constitute happiness. The true power of happiness is not ephemeral, it is transcendent. Contained in this book are lessons I learned from the animals, lessons that will help us cultivate happiness as a lifestyle. In fact, our brains are already wired to seek it. These lessons will guide us in reconnecting to our innate drive lying dormant within every one of us.

If that is the case, what stops us from being happy? For many of us, it's the pain we feel navigating through life experiences. It comes in all sorts of ways: betrayal, narcissism, victimhood, and abandonment. These things often leave us shattered. Some of us suffer because we feel invisible or overpowered, or we grieve the loss of a loved one or our own sovereignty, or perhaps we believe we are not enough, unworthy, small, or even unloved.

Many of us seek solace in religious dogma that provides hope. However, the binding rules of religion leave us with a sense of unworthiness when we are unable to abide by them. Some of us seek answers in the science of the psyche just to realize happiness becomes more and more elusive, the more knowledge we acquire. Many of us continue to search for answers outside of ourselves.

What if the answers we seek are within us already? What if all we need is a little guidance to find our way within? This book is the manual I always wished I had to help me navigate through life gracefully, a book that offers a methodology to bring our shattered heart pieces back together and be able to keep thriving in spite of it all.

Our deepest desire is to stop hiding our shattered heart behind the facade of strength. Deep down, we want to stop pushing through life carrying this pain everywhere we go. Some of us hope nobody sees our pain because if they do, we feel we may instantly fall apart. Some of us run from the pain and toward all sorts of unhealthy and self-destructive escape mechanisms. Many of us can't even endure the pain, so we harden our hearts to stop feeling, but in doing so, we stop feeling joy too. And some of us give up on life completely.

What if there is a book that provides instructions on how to understand the meaning beyond the darkness? What if instead we can learn to harness a transformative wisdom resulting in a more joyful human experience? What if *this* is the book that helps us break the cycle of pain once and for all?

The steps to happiness in this book do not come from me: it's the wisdom from the animals who taught me lessons with their unconditional love. Don't worry! **This book is not about pain**. It is not about working through heart wounds as a psychotherapy book would. It is not a hero's journey either. This book is not going to make you rationalize the causes of your traumas. No.

Wisdom, not ignorance, is bliss. Through a series of daily steps, we will explore the art of going within to cultivate our very own personal and unique recipe for a happier life. We each have a personal energetic signature that is interwoven in this collective tapestry we call life, making wisdom easier to access than you can imagine! These stories of the animals will illustrate the steps and show us what we can change inside us or in our lives. It may seem subtle at first, but over time, the transformation is unquestionable.

The wisdom shared by animals will help us perceive the world from the lens of love, changing it as a result. Perception *is* reality. Children inherently know this, and they, unlike adults, view the world with the eyes of innocence. They see love all around them. How can we as adults, reconnect to this childlike innocent perception? Animals are the key. They open our hearts and, in doing so, they help us open a portal to a liminal space of oneness. It is the dimension that transcends the constraints of time and space where we are one, we are whole, and where we are pure love. Yes, animals are the answer! This is why we love them so much!

Thanks to their wisdom, we can learn to be constantly bathed in the energy of unconditional love. It is the shift from living in the mind to living in the heart. This shift transforms pain to love, and struggle to thriving.

Animals are indeed sublime teachers of love. Those who cohabitate with us are masters at energy healing because they love us unconditionally, and through that love, we learn to be loving, and we learn to love others with an open heart. This is a true lesson on how to harness love as a force to change the energy within us and around us. Love is energy. Love heals. I hope together we enjoy this journey of harnessing our superpower—from identifying with our story to living our true self. My wish is to facilitate a shift to living life through the innocent perception of a child while we retain the wisdom of our adult self.

No matter our age, experiences, or background, happiness is within reach because it resides within us.

You may not have heard of energy healing before, and you may be wondering what this means. Or perhaps you are familiar with it, and you practice a certain modality already. Perhaps you are thinking, *This is outside of my comfort zone based on what I have been taught*, and you are thinking about putting this book down. Wherever you are in your understanding of energy healing, I invite you to read this book with the curiosity of a child learning something new for the very first time. I invite you to experience the joy of discovering a part of life you may have not given yourself permission to explore before. Today is the day. You have chosen this book because deep down you hear a little voice guiding you to tap fully into your inner power. I hope you read this through the eyes of your inner child, full of desire for learning every message the animals share in these pages.

Let me give you a quick example of energy healing to help you set aside for a moment any potential unconscious biases that may be lurking under the surface.

You may be having a very rough day. You are feeling down and beaten up, but you talk to a friend who then gives you a hug to help you feel better. After receiving that hug, the circumstances of your day have not changed, but suddenly your heart feels warm and fuzzy and somehow you feel a little less burdened. That is energy healing. A hug is a heart energy exchange between two people (or more). This is science. The average human being needs eight hugs daily to recharge their heart energy. Fewer hugs than that and mood disorders may start to creep up, just to mention one of the consequences of lack of heart energy. When fully charged, the heart has an extraordinary superpower. If you hug others and you witness how they feel better as a result, you are in fact witnessing the healing power of loving energy.

As you read through these pages, you will connect the dots on the power of love and how it is a healing force in the world. You will be able to embrace your power more fully. The animals' wisdom will help me illustrate energy healing in a way that makes sense. After all, animals have been incredible mentors in my life journey, and I imagine you will discover how they may have already been mentors in yours too.

Even though this is not a book about animal communication specifically, these instructions provide the foundation to open up to interspecies communication. It is in the space of love where communication on different levels takes place. Animals don't speak in words; they speak from the heart with energy. When we have developed a practice of being present in the heart, we can listen to them and to all of nature around us. It is the most authentic way of communicating because the message is never lost in the nuances of the spoken language, it is directly internalized in the feelings and emotions within the heart. It bypasses the mental workings of the brain, those unavoidable interpretations based on life experiences and goes directly to the heart. We can open the gateway of communication with animals. Understanding what animals have to say is a beautiful benefit to living in the energy of unconditional love.

You may be wondering why I chose to write this book now. Great question! It was a calling. I have navigated through intense pain three distinct times in my life where I felt I did not know how or if I was going to get through it. During these journeys, I was guided daily to shift perspectives one small step at a time until one day, I realized I had made it out of the darkness completely and back to myself again.

The situation that caused the pain had not gone away but my perspective of it had shifted and the pain was gone.

Similarly, it feels like we—all of humanity—are collectively going through a very dark night of the soul. I don't mean to say that it was any easier in any other time in history because from what I know and have read, past times were horrific in all sorts of ways. However, today as I write this book, there is a higher level of intensity I personally have not felt previously in my life, and I believe this is a time when we all need to truly get together as one and share the skills we excel at to get us through this challenging time together. **This is a time that calls for unity.** We are not alone. We are all in this together. And it is together, not individually, that we will all come to a better place.

Before we delve in, allow me to introduce you to my beloved animal companions without whom this book would not have been created. These mentors have chosen to live with me for the past ten-plus years: Luna, my bearded dragon, and Spikey, my terrier mix dog.

I find myself contemplating the messages I am sharing in my final manuscript. I am on my deck, relaxing in my lounge chair surrounded by what seems to be an infinite number of potted plants in bloom. A plethora of colors, textures and fragrances surround me. The trees above me are swaying with the gentle summer breeze, the hummingbirds are feeding from the abundance of flowers, and the sun is slowly setting, warming the left side of my face. It is truly a peaceful evening. Spikey is lounging right next to me and Luna is on my chest as I pet her softly through all those spikes that are part of her very interesting scaly, textured, reptile body. Unconditional loving energy is in the air, and it is almost palpable. In this moment, I am truly connected to the harmony of nature, the oneness of the universe, and the love of Spikey and Luna. All is well, and nothing else matters, only this now moment. I am fully present.

PREFACE

I notice in this moment of serenity, a little rainbow reflecting from a couple of Luna's scales around her neck. With curiosity, I see that the side of her body receiving the sun's rays reflects pastel tones of rainbow spirals. Every single spike on her body looks like a crystal pointer and at the very end of the spike is a rainbow spiral. I had never seen this on her body before.

When I try to touch each of those crystals and spirals, I realize that I can not. They are energy. It is her aura that I am seeing. Then I notice I can see my own aura as well—the same pastel colors that Luna has. Mine is a continuous line of minuscule rainbow orbs delineating the part of my body where the sun is shining. I also had never seen my own aura before, at least not in this way. It is fascinating trying to touch these minuscule orbs. I can't. They are not tangible; instead, there is a soft ethereal energy giving my body a rainbow-colored contour. Spikey's, however, is completely different.

He is surrounded by white geometric shapes, triangles, circles, and curved lines that envelop him in what seems to be a soft, white mist, like that of a cool, fall morning lingering above a calm stream or the soft mist that hovers over a silent meadow. As the sun sets, these auras are no longer visible to me. It was truly an evanescent magical moment.

Energy is real. Energy healing is also real. It is constantly happening all around us whether we take the time to see it and acknowledge it or not. I hope you embrace the stories in this book with an open heart because it is written with three fully open hearts: Luna's, Spikey's, and mine. It is the labor of our combined white and pastel, rainbow colored, unconditional loving energy that you are holding in your hands right now. Are we ready to embark on our superpower journey?

PART I
WHEN OUR HEARTS SHATTER

Emotional and physical pain are undeniable and can be equally damaging. In fact, broken heart syndrome is a medical term used to convey the physical pain felt in the heart during intensely painful emotional situations. It manifests as if the heart is experiencing a heart attack. It is not a pain to take lightly, and it can happen to anyone.

For many, the death of a loved one signifies their first real hurdle to happiness. Experiencing loss at an early age is especially devastating for the human mind. How do we comprehend the seeming finality of losing someone we love? There are so many types of pain, but this type of separation leaves our hearts shattered long-term.

We experience grief after a loved one's passing. It feels unbearable. However, we also may experience grief before they depart. Seeing death draw near is as emotionally devastating as the day of the final goodbye. How can we find comfort as we powerlessly see them fade away?

In addition to unbearable grief, with our beloved animals, we also have the added agonizing pain of not knowing when or if to make the decision of euthanizing them to reduce their imminent suffering. The burden of that choice is soul crushing too. I have seen how impossibly difficult it is for many to know exactly when the right time has come. It is quite challenging to be clear in our hearts to know without the shred of a doubt that the choice we make is the right one.

After all, we are their caregivers. We are their parents. We are the guardians they rely on for their basic needs, wants, and everything in between. This can feel overwhelming when their time to transition comes near. What if our animals can choose their time to go just like my grandma chose hers? It may seem outlandish at first, however, these following stories may help us open our mind to this possibility.

CROSSING THE RAINBOW BRIDGE

A dear friend of mine reached out to ask for my assistance with her cat's late senior years. She was getting signs that the time of his passing was coming. She was unclear whether to euthanize her cat to prevent further suffering or to allow things to follow their natural course, while minimizing his physical pain as much as possible. Does this situation sound familiar?

I connected with her cat and soon realized he was not wanting to depart yet. He wanted one last summer to enjoy the warmth of the sunlight on his fur. He was not moving much at that point, so it was not a question of going outside to hunt. It was more about enjoying the simple pleasure of appreciating the sun and the birds while being indoors.

This cat had good and bad days. Understandably, during those bad days my friend felt torn. *Is it time now? Am I being a bad mom for wanting to keep him with me longer even though it is clear he is suffering?*

And then the next day he would have another good day, and she was even more confused about what to do. I am sure we all can relate to this dilemma—at least those of us who have had senior animals under our care. We feel tasked with the seemingly impossible responsibility of doing the right thing. But how can we know for sure if we are indeed doing the right thing?

I gave her a simple solution to this dilemma: Allow the cat to decide when he wants to go. Ask him to tell you with an unequivocal message when he is ready to depart.

My recommendation to her was this: "Ask him to give you a clear sign of 'Now I am ready.' It may be as he refuses movement for three consecutive days, or skips two days of food, or anything else completely out of his character. It could be his not drinking any water, which is something that has never happened, or maybe doing his business in a place where he has never ever done it before. All of these can be his clear message. Just sit with your animal and ask, do one thing and one thing only and that way you will know the cat is telling you he is ready."

So, she did. She picked one of these suggestions. Her cat did not show the agreed behavior shared in his message right away. It was about a year later when finally, the sign was clear; she remembered, and immediately contacted me to verify this was true—he was ready. I connected with him again and yes, he was indeed ready to go and had no preference about being euthanized or not. He wanted to leave that up to her to decide what felt better for her. He wanted her to not agonize over his departure.

She scheduled for a vet to come to her house the next evening to put her beloved cat to sleep. Even though she already knew she had his permission to do so, she of course felt a heavy heart. The time had finally come to say goodbye. An hour before the vet was due to arrive, he passed away naturally in his loving home.

You see, each animal has a choice of when to depart. We can unburden ourselves from this overwhelming responsibility. We can simply ask the animal to tell us, just like the cat told my friend. What a liberating feeling it is, knowing that when we say goodbye it is truly their choice not ours. All we need to do is ask.

Animals do not see death the same way we do. A lot of us have been told through religious indoctrination that death is the end. Many of us also *know* this is not true. Animals also know it is not the end; therefore, they do not fear it the way many humans do. They know they will reunite with their loved ones who departed before them, and they look forward to the happy reunion. However, they are conflicted about their departure because they also know we will mourn them. They feel torn because they do not want to see us suffer. For this reason, many times we may get mixed signals regarding the exact moment our animal companion may wish to transition. This is why asking them what they want to do is critical for clearing ambiguity.

WHAT I LEARNED FROM THIS CAT

I get many questions from animals' guardians who need to know—Is it time? Is it *not* the right time? How do I know for sure? What I hear in my heart is actually this: *How can I know I am making the right decision for my beloved animal? I would not be able to live with the guilt of robbing my animal of a second of his life because I made the wrong decision.*

If this is you or someone you love, please remember this simple practice of asking your beloved animal for that one, single, clear sign, and you will not have to agonize over not knowing when the right time comes.

I hope this story brings peace in our hearts at a time when we feel heartbroken with the imminent physical separation. Yes, we will grieve and mourn their passing, which is already hard enough, but hopefully with this guidance, our decision will not add to the pain of our grieving process.

We have discussed a topic that affects us deeply—death. I know a thing or two about death. By age twenty-one, I had lost my father, my grandma, and a number of college, neighborhood, and school friends. I had seen more death than most nonmilitary people do at that age. The one that truly hit the hardest was the death of my grandma.

My beloved grandmother was the light of my life, and I was hers. When I was a kid, she consistently made me feel seen, heard, and therefore, immensely loved. Day after day, I would come from school and be part of her routine: cooking, cleaning, and caring for her chickens, her dove, her cat, her canary, and the rest of her menagerie. We would bake cookies and make bread from scratch, and we would sit and eat together while talking about my day and hers. She would listen to me with great love in her heart. I could tell hearing about my day brought life into her golden years.

She never left the house. She had advanced arthritis and walking was too painful. She stayed home to limit her walking as much as possible. I was an intrinsic part of her life just like she was in mine. I felt valued, appreciated, and unlike many kids at this age, I felt useful and accomplished because I knew that thanks to my help, her life was better. My life as a kid was so full of purpose thanks to her. She gave me that invaluable gift. There were other relatives in my life, but I did not connect with them as deeply as I connected with my grandma.

During the last couple of years of her life I cared for her at home when she was bedridden. As her final day got closer, she had already transitioned to another realm, where she consistently talked to her mother and her best friend, a deceased neighbor who before her passing, used to visit her every day. She talked to other relatives of hers whom I had never met. I would enter the room, and she would not know my name. I remember how sad I felt that the person I loved most in the world did not know who I was anymore. However, I took comfort in knowing all these souls were in the room with her welcoming her to the afterlife. That was clearly what was happening. She had one foot in this world and the other foot in another realm.

The day she chose to depart, I remember it was my turn to stay with her. We took turns, her son, her cousin, and me. We were a team of three looking after her. Sunday night on August 21, decades back, was my shift. I told the other two relatives I did not want them to leave me alone because I knew she was going to transition. I begged until I convinced them to stay. They were exhausted from taking care of her the previous nights, so they were looking forward to sleeping in their beds, in their own homes. Deep down they knew that if I was right, they would regret not being there on her final night to say goodbye. So, they stayed.

My grandma's breathing became more labored. She already had an oxygen mask, but she was not breathing well. By 9 p.m., her room was packed with relatives who came to say goodbye. They stayed with her for a couple of hours: her children, grandchildren, people I saw regularly, as well as people I rarely encountered in my day-to-day, were all there. But she did not die. They left late at night. Then my uncle said it might be a good idea if I said goodbye to her. I was finally left alone in the room with her. They all went to sleep. I talked to her from my heart. I did not think she would know who I was, but I did not let that stop me. I told her how much I loved her; how grateful I was that she was the person who raised me and loved me unconditionally. I had not realized until that moment that she was not able to leave because of me. I told her I was going to be fine. She had raised me to be resourceful, smart, and strong, and I knew how to take care of myself.

As I mentioned earlier, I was only twenty-one. I did not know how I was going to live without her, but I knew that somehow, I would figure it out. I reassured her many times all would be well and that she could leave in peace, and I would make it. She always took pride in how smart I was so I reminded her that indeed I would be quite capable of figuring it all out. Without making eye contact, without uttering a word, I knew she heard me. It was midnight. I held her hand as I finished telling her this, and I just stayed in her bed trying to rest a little because I was tired too. It had been an emotional night for all of us, especially for me, because I knew this was the day she would leave us. It was only one hour later, at 1:20 a.m., when she exhaled her last breath as I watched her and held her hand. She chose to pass away once everyone but me had left the room.

What an honor it was for me to be there to see her transition to a beautiful place. I saw her expression change from agony to bliss. One look at her and I knew she was in a happy place. I could not even cry, I was so relieved to know she was finally in peace and without pain, reunited with all her loved ones with whom she had been talking for the past few months. The person I loved the most in this world had now departed.

Transitioning to the other side is not the end of being. It is only the end of our physical form. Animals showed me how to communicate with loved ones on the other side. To this day, I connect with my grandmother regularly. I don't *believe* she is with me; I *know* she is. I'm as certain as I know my name is Stephanie. Some might say our loved ones become our guardian angels, and there is some truth to that. They are watching over us after all. They are proud of our accomplishments, and they are supporting us through our challenges. **They leave us physically, but they stay with us spiritually**.

What I did not know then is that animals can be a bridge to communicate with our departed loved ones. The people we love sometimes choose to show themselves in the form of an animal. Even for one fleeting moment, they want to connect with us in the physical realm.

You may be wondering what animal my grandma has chosen to send messages through to me. Here is a little interesting fact: My grandma was an animal lover in her own right. She had a menagerie of animals in her home and backyard. Over the years I took care of ducks, geese, chickens, a dove, a canary, fish, and two cats. All of them were hers. The connection I have with animals is strong, because every animal I connect with unites me with the love of my grandmother. I followed her lead when it came to learning the language of animals. Each animal shows us love differently. I learned this while taking care of her animals. She was my first teacher on how to open my heart to love and be loved unconditionally by all these beautiful beings. It is my energy healing practice that connects me with my grandma every single day. Not one animal but all of them. She deepened the connection between me and the animal kingdom. For that and for everything else she gave me and continues to give me, I am infinitely grateful.

Perhaps you have experienced or are experiencing the pain of losing a loved one—human or animal, the pain seems unbearable no matter who it is. I hope my story lays a foundation for what is possible. Sometimes, animals come to give us messages from loved ones. Sometimes, animals give us messages from Spirit, so we are reminded to shift perspectives and get out of our thoughts and back into our hearts. This story from the hummingbirds for instance shows how we can extract meaning out of what on the surface may appear as just a tiny little encounter. I am here to tell you: **No animal encounter is ever without a deeper meaning**.

HUMMINGBIRDS

Many people connect with hummingbirds in a special way. They might be the reminder of a loved one who has passed. But for me, hummingbirds bring another message. They are these gorgeous, iridescent birds that mesmerize me with their ever-changing colors.

They are a beautiful marvel of nature. They remind me to see the world from a different perspective—from above, as if I am watching a movie, my own movie. They remind me to be joyful like they are when hopping from flower to flower. They are to me the bird version of a dolphin: always happy, always playful!

One year, I had a series of quite extraordinary experiences with hummingbirds. As I sat out on the deck, a hummingbird would feed from my flowers, and then before leaving, it would come over and hover inches away from my face. I always felt a sense of gratitude coming from it. It was a hello and a message of thanks.

On another occasion, a hummingbird hovered inches away from my face as I was walking my dog, Spikey, on the trail. There were no flowers nearby that I could see. The hummingbird came seemingly out of nowhere and just hovered close to my face for quite some time, so much so that I was very intrigued about why that would happen. As I connected to the message from this hummingbird, I learned it was the friend of a friend who had recently passed away. This time, it was a friend coming to say hello. She was a very sweet lady, and I enjoyed her company every time we met at our friend's house. Her passing made me sad. I did not have a chance to say goodbye. So, there she was, saying hello and using the body of a hummingbird to come to me. What a sweet moment! Now, I too have had an experience with hummingbirds that reminds me of a loved one.

My moments with hummingbirds continued. I would be walking with Spikey and would encounter as many as seven hummingbirds in about a quarter of a mile area with no flowers. I always found that quite bizarre. After all, they need to constantly eat so what were they doing using their time to say hello rather than searching for food? The answer was, they were very diligently reminding me to keep seeing life from a different perspective like they do. Every time I would be loving the moment, loving the trees on the trail, loving the fresh air I was breathing, loving the sunlight of the long days of summer, they hovered in front of me for several seconds. Not all at once. One at a time. It was so mesmerizing.

WHAT HUMMINGBIRDS HAVE TAUGHT ME

I have learned to shift my perspective on my own, so I do not let life bring me down for too long. I know I can shift my perspective just like the hummingbirds go from flower to flower. Sometimes it takes me longer than others, but I always manage to shift the way I see things. My goal is to remember I am the observer of my own story, detaching myself from the situation that causes me pain and seeing it from above.

If you are dealing with the loss of a loved one, perhaps ask them to connect with you through an animal. Perhaps it's a hummingbird, but maybe it's another creature that you both appreciated very much. You have nothing to lose and so much to gain! Would you consider giving it a try? Is there a loved one in your life who is preparing to transition? Why not agree ahead of time on what animal they love so when they have departed, you will know it is them visiting when you see that animal? Wouldn't that be one of the most comforting feelings in the world knowing without a doubt they do visit you? To know with certainty they are still with you? I personally find it very comforting. After all, death is not the end. It is a transition to another realm where loved ones still exist. From there, they can still connect with those who remain behind. The question is, are we ready to acknowledge their visits?

Perhaps now death does not sound so finite. Maybe the wound of loss can be lessened just a little bit with this knowledge. Perhaps hummingbirds can be a reminder to change perspectives, to remember that life does continue after death.

YES! It is possible to live a happy life after enduring the pain of grief. We can put our hearts back together after being shattered. The strategies in this book are what made my heart whole again. If I found my joy after losing my grandma, imagine what this manual could do for you.

After covering the topic of shifting perspectives regarding our grieving hearts, how about diving into the infinite loving power that resides within? What exactly does this mean? Perhaps you are wondering if it is the love of a partner, a spouse, a child, or a friend? It is far more than what labels can explain. It is a force. It is an intelligence. It can be harnessed with intention, and if we don't heal from our inner pain, we can also unintentionally dim this power to imperceptible levels.

In the next chapter, I invite you to dive into the power of unconditional love energy. How can we discern thoughts from feelings and how does it translate into energy? And what exactly is energy anyway? We hear of this law of physics but how does this manifest in our day-to-day existence? If you are ready to discover this with the curiosity of a child's innocent perception, let's continue, shall we?

PART 2
THE HEART IS THE KEY

Let's pause for a moment and take a deep breath. Pay attention to how that felt. Did it give you a moment to connect with yourself even if it was brief?

Before we learn how to be happier versions of ourselves, we need to learn who we truly are. Who are we? We are not our names, what we do, or where we live. It is worth stopping to reassess what we *believe* we are or what we have been told we are supposed to be. Once we understand who we are, we can flow into a better version of ourselves more gracefully. Breath is the anchor to bring us within and rediscover our true selves, an act so simple and yet so profound, as I will explain next.

In 2006, I came across *The New Earth* by Eckhart Tolle. At the time, I was a typical career woman: raising a child, trying to keep things together, and carrying a very fast pace in life with too many responsibilities and too little time to decompress. Tolle's book profoundly changed me in a way I could never have imagined. I learned the importance of presence. What a gift! I regained control of my life by allowing pauses to organically flow within my day. I was finally able to disconnect from my mental chatter and connect with myself.

Presence, it turns out, is a superpower! All it took was ten minutes each day. No agenda, no to-do list, no task. I just sat, closed my eyes, and breathed.

Once I cultivated presence in my daily life, I was able to take it a step further. A complete paradigm shift unfolded next. Tolle explained that we are *not* the roles (role of mother, professional, student, friend, daughter, etc.) we play in life. We are *not* the titles or positions or status we have, and we are not anything material that the eye can see. We are the awareness that observes it all: thoughts, emotions, actions, feelings, and more. **We are *the* presence that is aware of it *all*.**

This presence is infinite and the way it feels to me is unconditional love.

Let's pause, take another deep breath, and sit for a few seconds with that truth.

This is who we truly are: unconditional love! Expansive, blissful, infinite love.

This transformed my life forever. I stopped identifying with the roles of the external world. I love all my activities, including my job, hobbies, and relationships. But I learned to find myself in the stillness of my presence, not in the roles I play. As I continued to practice being present, I started connecting with myself at a deeper level. I learned that the heart, not the mind, is the key to tapping into this higher power. It was by tuning in to my heart that I could connect with my soul, with Spirit. All ancient, worldwide teachings practice stillness to connect within. You may have heard the words *meditation, mindfulness,* or *prayer*. They all refer to the practice of being still and connecting within, and it is in this stillness that our hearts open the gate so this infinite, unconditional love can be felt. It is an ineffable state of bliss.

PART 2: THE HEART IS THE KEY

You may be wondering why we often feel like the mind is the one controlling our existence. We are incessantly thinking, but what role does the mind play? Here is what I have learned in my practice. **The heart is the seat of the spirit, and the brain is the seat of the mind**. The heart navigates our existence through emotions, feelings, perceptions, and impressions. The mind navigates our physical presence in the world through thoughts and mental processes. The heart carries an inherent inner wisdom which comes from being the home of the soul. The mind acquires knowledge (data) through deduction, inference, analysis, and memorization. Our existence is a harmonious balance between these two main agents that drive all we are and all we do while in human form. When we are not thriving, it means the heart or the mind or the relationship between the two is out of balance.

This is what I have to say about the mind and our heart in relation to who we truly are. However, I would like to bring in the actual experts in the realm of psychology studies of the mind to provide a quick overview of what they discovered through their careers. Who are we in essence? The terminology may be a bit different from mine: mind/heart versus mind/consciousness, but with their interpretation of the mind and consciousness, we can then start putting the pieces of the puzzle together. Who are we? What is the mind? And what does it mean when I say, the heart is the key? The key to what? Let's find out!

Carl Jung, one of the cofounders of modern analytical psychology, is a well-known psychology luminary. Many textbooks studied in psychology degrees around the world are based on his analysis of the psyche, the mind. What is less known in mainstream, however, is that Jung was quite a spiritual man. One of his works was the theory of individuation, the process of understanding what self is and is not. Jung studied the mind at length, and he realized through his research that we go through three different kinds of births. Everyone will have two births, but not all will experience all three. We are first born in physical form; second, we are born again when we have an ego that gets separated from the environment; and the third time we are born is when we reach spiritual consciousness.

In his studies of the mind, he realized there was more to being than our ego, which is a construct of the mind. He studied multiple religions to learn more about the transcendence of self. He wanted to find ways to reach mental well-being. It is quite interesting to see that one of the most erudite psychologists in history discovered through his life's research that we are not our minds. And yet, here we are—many of us are still identifying ourselves with what our minds tell us we are. What else did Jung discover in his anthropological, religious, philosophical, psychiatric, literary, and archaeological studies? I am both fascinated by his work and his conclusions regarding what we are beyond our minds. No wonder his research bridged psychology with spirituality. Carl Jung developed psychotherapy models and psychological analysis that helped birth a branch of psychology that studies human consciousness beyond the mind: transcendence psychology.

Another brilliant therapist, who on the other hand specializes in psychiatry, is Brian Weiss MD. He has decades of psychiatric experience, and through sessions with his patients, he also learned quite empirically that his patients were in fact a consciousness transcending the limits of time and space beyond the constructs of the mind. More precisely, he was able to arrive at this conclusion by seeing what unfolded when he treated his patients through life regression. He successfully dissolved untreatable phobias his patients were suffering from which originated in previous lives. His patients were also able to overcome traumas rooted in previous lifetimes which were impeding them from carrying on functional lives. When I read *Many Lives, Many Masters* as an adolescent, it was Weiss' learnings through therapy that corroborated for me a knowing I always had: We transcend the limits of the mind. How fascinating! This truth is supported by one of the most experienced and renowned psychiatrists of our time. Brian Weiss studied at Yale School of Medicine, New York University Medical Center, and Columbia University and has had an extensive career as the Head of Psychiatry at Mount Sinai Medical Center in Miami.

Based on my practice and based on the discoveries of these mind experts, **we are consciousness.** In my own words, **we are unconditional love.** I will refer to these two terms interchangeably. How do we access our higher level of consciousness if it is beyond the constructs of the mind? This is where our hearts come into play. This is how this works. Let's deconstruct this truth step by step.

Albert Einstein said that all in the universe is energy, and this includes us. Based on what I have learned in my energy healing practice, our hearts have a dual function when it comes to energy. **Our hearts are the receptors and transmitters connecting us to all of creation.** Perhaps you may refer to all of creation using other words such as the I AM presence, Source, Spirit, Oneness, Consciousness, or God.

We each are a little spark of Oneness: each equally important, each equally precious sparks of Consciousness (each person, each animal, each plant, each drop of water, each stone…). It is through the heart that we connect with all other sparks of Oneness. What exactly does the heart do when it comes to connecting us to one another, to Source?

Perhaps this analogy will bring clarity to this truth. Some of us were born before this millennium and we had the opportunity of owning a dial radio. Not a digital one or a satellite one or an app on our phone (those did not exist back then), but a physical device that had a dial that we turned to the left or to the right. We used this to tune to the frequency from which our favorite radio station was transmitting. If we did not tune *exactly* to that frequency, we heard garbled noise or even pure static. When we tuned to the right frequency, we could hear music being transmitted by the radio tower only through that specific frequency of radio waves (for example, 102.7 FM or 503 AM). There are two types of radio wave frequencies typically used: FM (frequency modulation) and AM (amplitude modulation). The first is less prone to interference while the latter is a stronger and more constant signal. We operate like a radio station. We each have our very own specific frequency—just like the radio towers transmit the frequency of their radio stations. Similarly, we each transmit our frequency to those around us.

Those of us born in this millennium are far more familiar with the wireless fidelity frequency commonly known as Wi-Fi. These are the radio waves used by current technology to connect to the world wide web often referred to as internet. A vast majority of electronic devices we use daily are connected to Wi-Fi. We may have noticed how the frequency weakens or gets stronger based on our geographical location. We can see the bars in our phone decrease as we get farther away from the tower it connects to. In contrast, we can also see the bars go up as our phone gets closer to the tower and the frequency signal intensifies making the connection to our device stronger. We see this in our computers, phones, and other devices. Frequency is not a foreign term for us. We heavily depend on it to carry out our day-to-day lives. I personally cannot do my job if I can't connect to the internet. Frequency is part of our lives whether we believe in it or not. It is as real as we are. Many of us know this very well.

The heart operates in a similar way. Our hearts tune into frequencies of energy emitted by everything around us: animate and inanimate objects, nature, animals, people, and manufactured objects alike. **Everything carries a frequency because everything is energy.** This frequency, just like the radio stations and Wi-Fi, varies in strength.

There are strong signals and there are weak signals. Some are pure garble, and some are pristine music to the soul. The higher frequencies are the ones that lift our spirit. The lower frequencies bring us down.

Our emotions are the indicators used to identify high or low frequencies. As mentioned earlier the heart has a dual function. Besides having the function of a transmitter, the heart also acts as a receptor, tuning into the frequencies like a radio does. Of course, like the radio, we cannot hear all radio stations at once. Like Wi-Fi, we can't connect to *all* available networks at once. The heart needs to focus its attention and intention on one frequency at a time. Once our heart chooses what to focus on, that is the energy we will be able to receive.

At the same time, the heart is a transmitter. Once we have tuned into the preferred frequency, the heart transmits it throughout the entire body. Frequency is carried through the intricate electrical network called the nervous system. Every organ, every cell, every muscle, every bone, and every tissue vibrate to the frequency we have tuned ourselves to. Imagine coming home late at night to a dark house. We turn on the light and the entire place is illuminated: the floor, the furniture, the decor, the plants, and the ceiling. Frequency works in our body in a similar way. The frequency we connect to illuminates or dims every cell of our body in the same way a bright light or dimmed light illuminates a dark room.

As a transmitter, the heart projects the frequency it is tuned to in the same way a megaphone projects sound, broadcasting it all around. The frequency we broadcast is usually not heard with our ears but felt in our heart, and it is processed mentally by the subconscious mind. Some people can hear frequencies; it is a subtle ringing in the ear that can be perceived when we are in complete stillness, like an imperceptible humming sound. That is our own frequency. I can hear mine during my meditations.

The heart is in fact the most spectacular receptor and transmitter ever created! I marvel every single day at how the heart has this tremendous power to change and transform everything around us based on the frequency it is tuned into. The key to living a blissful life is becoming proficient at keeping the heart tuned into the frequency of love. This is what makes us feel uplifted.

Cultivating presence every day allows us to listen to the heart. Our heart is the key to connecting us to a higher consciousness or to a lower consciousness. It is all about what frequency we choose to connect to. When we develop the ability to discern which frequency we are tuned into every moment of the day, we can constantly be the best version of ourselves. It is all about frequency.

Our hearts have the key to identifying frequencies. It is not complicated. We all are quite familiar with emotions. **Each emotion is a frequency.** We will delve more deeply into how to acquire and refine the skill of being accountable for our emotions in the following chapter.

Now that we have a better understanding of how the heart is the key to connecting to our consciousness, let's discuss frequencies more in depth. In order to find the right station for our heart to tune into, we need to understand what constitutes high and low frequencies and how they translate into how we feel. How we feel will then dictate how we think, communicate, and act in the world. How we act in the world will shape the energetic signature we transmit to ourselves and to others. Having this understanding will open the door to a better version of ourselves, one that is more loving and more self-actualized.

The topic of frequency has been extensively studied by scientists, physicists, and mathematicians for centuries. Nikola Tesla for example said, **"If you want to find the secrets of the universe, think in terms of energy, frequency, and vibration."** His quote sums up quite well what I have personally experienced. I hope my message here translates this concept into how this is lived by every single one of us on Earth, every single day: humans, animals, trees, plants, insects, rocks, mountains, lakes, and oceans, and all of creation alike.

First, I would like to share a couple of stories from insects that were clear examples of how all of creation, not just humans, receives the energy we transmit. We may or may not be aware of what frequency we are tuned to, but nature and humans feel it, and they respond to it in ways I personally find incredibly magical.

A few years back, I went to celebrate Memorial weekend with a group of friends at a friend's house in a beautiful area surrounded by a forest. Of course, living in Oregon, we have so much moisture in the soil that slugs are always present in our yards, fields, and forests.

But this particular time, I came across a slug, and it was a revelation to me. As I was leaving my friend's house with two friends, a slug was on the step and was heading from our right to our left. We stopped. We admired the size of this gigantic slug. (Some may cringe reading this.) I do not have any aversion towards slugs, so to me, it was amazing to see how big it was. Pure admiration. My body was clearly vibrating at a high frequency of love for this being that I was admiring intensely. The slug received my frequency so clearly that it changed direction. Instead of continuing to move towards our left, the slug made a ninety-degree turn and started moving directly towards me.

What did I learn from this seemingly inconsequential moment? All of creation, insects included, has a level of sentience that can navigate energy fields and discern higher frequencies from lower ones. Nature, and its divine essence, never ever ceases to amaze me. What a marvel of creation we live in!

I have another example of how the smallest beings visibly respond to frequency. I may need to preface this little story with the fact that

I love all animals, feathery, furry, scaly, spiky, and slimy too! This is a very fun story.

I was on a spiritual retreat a few years back in Mount Shasta. A dozen people from different places in the US had come to Mt. Shasta to connect to the land and meditate and create a community during a beautiful summer week.

In fact, we all were meditating under the falls one day when, to my surprise, not one but two small, slimy creatures came out of the rocks and started making their way toward our group. Much like the slug, they intentionally came from their safe hideout to get closer to us.

I had only seen salamanders maybe once or twice in my life and never up close. I was not familiar with how they looked or where they typically lived. I was very intrigued by this unexpected appearance. Since our group respects life, we did not try to overwhelm the salamanders by having a dozen humans towering over their tiny little bodies to observe them. We continued our meditation, and these tiny little beings continued to move several feet in our direction. They were quite literally an arm's length from us. They specifically chose to come to us. They felt our collective frequency and wanted to tune into it like we humans tune into a radio station we like or the Wi-Fi network we prefer.

I quickly went toward the salamanders and picked them up and returned them to the same spot under the rock they came from to keep them safe from harm. There were several hikers nearby and we feared they would be crushed.

What I learned from this story was that animals of all types respond to frequency. During meditation, our energy is amplified, and we are a much louder megaphone that transmits an uplifting frequency—not just to us but to everyone around us. Animals love to be part of this loving energy our hearts exude when in a peaceful state.

This is why the salamanders came out of hiding and made their way toward us. When we are aware of the positive or not so positive effect of the frequency we transmit, we can then make a better effort at cultivating more peace in our hearts. This way we can be in and exude peace so others can feel it in our presence. It is a domino effect, really. We have more power to change the world we live in than we give ourselves credit for.

To summarize, the heart is a receiver and a transmitter of frequencies that, like radio waves, can be received and felt by those around us. We have also learned from professionals of the mind that we are more than our thoughts: We are consciousness. We also have discussed how the heart can help us navigate the infinite sea of frequency waves that together represent our energetic footprint in this world. That is who we truly are, and in the core of it all is our essence: unconditional love.

I mentioned earlier that animate and inanimate objects carry frequencies. All of creation does. This includes inanimate objects created by our own hands or by machines in factories. I have experienced this truth in many occasions. Here is an earlier experience, where I witnessed it in my own home.

I have had a Buddha statue as my meditation companion for the past two decades. This Buddha represents the energy of peace. I look at it and I am reminded to look within and find my center. This statue has been in many rooms in my house bringing me a sense of serenity through the many storms I have weathered.

One day, I recall going to the farmers' market and buying two identical bouquets of flowers to take home to beautify the space and bring a smile to my face. I placed one bouquet next to the Buddha. As the days went by, I changed the water in both vases and kept admiring the beauty of the flowers. Flowers not only make the space more beautiful, but also, they carry the frequency of happiness. I noticed that after a week or so the flowers close to me started to wither. *That is quite normal*, I thought; they are not meant to last forever. However, when I looked at the flowers by the Buddha statue, they looked like they were not a day older than the day I brought them home. In fact, two weeks passed, and they were still vibrant, while the others had already died. In fact, this bouquet lasted twice as long as the other one. The only difference was the Buddha's proximity. Clearly this Buddha statue was emitting a higher frequency, and the flowers responded to it by living twice as long.

Just imagine the frequency of different world religions' paintings or statues revered by millions of people around the world. If one small Buddha statue has such a powerful effect, just imagine the high frequency they must transmit.

I hope this Buddha experience gives you some insight into how our world is energy vibrating at different frequencies at all times, whether it is a living being or an inanimate object.

This is now the time to delve deeper into the concept of frequencies. Another renowned psychiatrist of our era, Sir Dr. David R. Hawkins, published a book in 2006 called *Transcending the Levels of Consciousness: The Stairway to Enlightenment*, which for the first time brought to the Western world what Indigenous people, Aborigines, and the First and Second Nation peoples have known for ages.

Our emotions have different frequencies. **The more positive the emotion we experience, the higher the frequency we transmit**. The opposite is also true: The lower the frequency, the lower the emotion. The higher emotions bring well-being while the lower emotions translate into disease (mental and physical). As humans, the sea of emotions we navigate daily brings about a never-ending wave of high and low frequencies. It is all based on our emotional responses to the happenings of the day. This gamut of emotions is what constitutes the Map of Consciousness that in other words can be translated into our sense of self. Dr. Hawkins' work is groundbreaking for those of us who did not grow up connected to the frequency of the land through ancient native practices, ceremonies, and culture. The peoples of the world who have been in direct connection to the land have always known frequencies, even though they do not refer to them using that term.

Navigating our emotions, we are able to connect to our true self. No wonder our heart is that key we need to open the door to our superpower. It is through our heart that we experience what it is like to exist. It is through our heart we can find the path to take and the path to avoid based on the experiences we want to have. **Our heart is our life's compass**.

I love what Matt Kahn, spiritual author, once said: **"The name of the game is to find our way back to love."** When we get heartbroken, we need to find our way back to love. When we get lied to, we need to find our way back to love. When we experience grief, again, we need to find our way back to love—not love *of* someone in particular but the frequency of love in the heart. We can experience life events both good and not so good and be able to recalibrate our emotions to bring us back to a loving and harmonious state of being. This quote from Matt Kahn is what I tell myself when I experience an unpleasant event. My job is to not dwell on the lower emotion but to find my way back to a loving state of being again. That is truly what our mission in life is all about: living through it all and still coming back to a place of loving presence. Our hearts lead the way.

Please do not get me wrong. I am not saying to always be in a harmonious state of being no matter the circumstances. No. **Having emotions is what makes us human**. We experience grief, betrayal, disappointment, resentment, guilt, sadness, and so many other emotions that make up our truth in any given moment. We need to learn to come back to harmony. Every time. Regardless of the situation. That is the difference. It means, if we experience betrayal once, we must not carry that feeling of betrayal with us all our life. Absolutely not. It means we should face the emotion, feel it, let it run through our system, and then release it like a dove in the wind to fly away from us into the horizon. We know we have not released an emotion when similar life circumstances trigger us and bring us back to the moment when that emotion was first felt. I highly recommend reading the book *The Emotion Code* by Dr. Bradley Nelson. I guarantee we will never underestimate the effect of our emotions on our bodies after learning what this renowned holistic medicine physician has to say on this topic.

All we need to do is to come back to love like Matt Kahn says. Come back to a harmonious state of being. This sounds so simple and yet it is far from easy, as I am sure we all know very well. It requires daily practice to achieve this level of expertise. The blissful result of this practice makes the effort unquestionably worth it.

Our current Dalai Lama once said: **"Our mission in life is to be happy."** When we rebalance our emotions, the energy that is transmitted through our hearts is the essence of what we are—unconditional love. Our mission in life is staying balanced and in a state of happiness so we can then share that energy with the world too. That is quite the job. This means **we need to be responsible for our own emotions,** not only for ourselves but for everyone else's sake too. We do create the world around us based on what frequency we emanate most of the time. In other words, if a person we encounter somewhere was in a bad mood and says something we don't like, wouldn't that affect our day? Many of us may like to use the excuse of having a bad day, but don't we all have bad days? The difference is **emotional accountability; we don't want our bad day to become someone else's**

bad day too. That is the key! In order to start owning our emotions and the impact they have on ourselves and those around us, it is now time to really learn about frequencies more in depth.

WHAT ARE FREQUENCIES?

As mentioned earlier Dr. David R. Hawkins studied emotions and was able to measure a specific hertz range for each. He published multiple books on this subject, including the international bestselling book titled *Power vs. Force* and *The Map of Consciousness Explained: A Proven Energy Scale to Actualize Your Ultimate Potential.* These books outline his scientific approach to measuring human emotions. His method transformed the concept of human emotions from subjective to objective. There is a specific hertz frequency range associated with each emotion that makes them quite distinct from one another. Let me share a few.

From top to bottom

700+ Hz	Enlightenment
600 Hz	Peace
540 Hz	Joy
500 Hz	Love
400 Hz	Reason
350 Hz	Acceptance
310 Hz	Willingness
250 Hz	Neutrality
200 Hz	Courage
175 Hz	Pride
150 Hz	Wrath
125 Hz	Desire

100 Hz	Fear
75 Hz	Grief
50 Hz	Apathy
30 Hz	Guilt
20 Hz	Shame

According to his research explained in *The Map of Consciousness*, 87 percent of the population is positioned around 207 Hz which is neutrality and courage. According to Dr. Hawkins, we want to ideally be in the 500 Hz range, which is the frequency of love and joy. **This range of 500 Hz and above is what keeps us in a healthier state, mentally, emotionally, and physically.** The frequencies of below 500 Hz can be precursors of disease.

His exceptional lifelong career in psychiatric medicine and his discoveries have earned him numerous recognitions around the world just like the professionals of the mind cited earlier. I am glad a professional of his caliber was able to document and scientifically prove something that we all inherently know already.

I invite us all to test our frequency by visiting a place where there is a group of animals (for example a dog park) and to observe how the dogs respond to our energy based on how we feel in that moment. If we need ideas on how to achieve this, I can share one of the ways I work on uplifting my frequency as I start the day. I wake up in the morning and first thing I do is meditate. My energy is peaceful when I wake up. After meditating, I am vibrating at a higher frequency before I leave my house. At the dog park, I practice gratitude. The thoughts running in my mind while I am at the park are all about gratitude for everything around me: the water that brings life, the air that sustains life to all beings, the warmth of the sun that makes life possible, and the ground I am standing on that supports us all. This frequency of gratitude is quite magnetic. Dogs come and greet me regardless of their breed. They are not coming for treats; I carry no food with me. They come because they respond to a nurturing frequency.

Just this week a little pug (one I had never seen before) jumped on my bench to get on my lap. Her human had to come and pick her up from my lap because she would not come to her. She wanted to be with me. A husky who was across the field—probably not a young one—slowly, but with a determined pace, walked directly to me. Again, another dog I had never seen before made all that effort to come be in my presence. Then a caramel Lab, who was playful and young, also jumped on my bench and wanted to give me kisses. Out of all the people in the dog park, the Lab picked me to be the recipient of all this affection. Before I knew it, I had about five different dogs around me and I had no treats. It was my energy they were responding to. My visits to the dog park are a true demonstration of how my frequency is received. I owe it to them and to everyone on my path to share the most positive energy I can harness. I know they feel it. I have clear evidence of it. They all are a reminder of the importance of owning our emotions and working on finding our way back to love when we are unbalanced.

The best way to know what energy we are transmitting into the world is by checking in with the thoughts percolating in our mind. We are always in control of our mind; all it takes is awareness and we can shift our thoughts. **Animals can help us take accountability of our frequency**. Let's allow them to teach us how to become proficient with how we manage our energy. The more aware we become, the easier it is to stay at a higher frequency for longer periods of time.

Have you ever walked into an empty room and felt like you walked into something? It's so palpable and tangible that you feel the discomfort even though no one is there? Your heart undoubtedly picked up on the residue of an altercation, a fight, or a heated debate that had transpired prior to your arrival. Let's say your body carried the range of around 207 Hz because you had spent your time in meditation and gratitude earlier that day, but the room still held the 150 Hz (or lower), the direct result of the anger, then shame, or the grief that the perpetrators left behind. This is not a fabrication of the mind. This is not fantastical. This is science.

I remember one day, years ago, I was visiting the headquarters of a past employer of mine. There were multiple buildings, and I walked into one of them—on the second floor specifically—and I felt an immediate sense of doom. My heart quite literally dropped, and a feeling of sadness invaded me. I did not know why but the feeling was incredibly oppressive; I wanted to turn around and leave. But I continued walking in there because I needed to see my customer, the purpose of my visit to this building. I then learned that someone had died by suicide the week before on the same floor. The frequency of despair which led the person to the act of suicide was still lingering in the space. My heart, my infallible receptor, picked up on the negative frequency the moment I stepped on that floor and my frequency dropped from wherever it was to a lower frequency of despair.

The opposite is also true. Don't we all love to go to a place where there are waterfalls, rivers, lakes, or the ocean? Anywhere around water really. The real estate industry knows this very well. Anyone who has ever acquired a home by the water knows the prices of houses are significantly higher because the proximity to the water adds value to the property. Why is that? Let me ask this question in a different way. Is it possible to feel angry or uncomfortable just by being near water?

When we are by the water, there is a sense of rejuvenation and revitalization that happens as if the water washes away all the lower frequencies we carry through our thoughts, our emotional wounds, and our day-to-day burdens. This is because the water, in its natural state, has a frequency that can feel exponentially higher than our average frequency. As a result, it has a recalibrating effect on our energetic field.

Higher frequency locations are prime vacation destinations because they make us feel good. It is not just taking time off work that makes us feel good, our frequency is being uplifted to a higher one through the elements of the Earth—in this case, the water element. The water element carries a very potent frequency indeed. That is precisely why we tend to gravitate toward bodies of water whenever we have the opportunity.

Have you noticed how many sacred sites (religious or ancient) are located by a well or a spring or a cove? I personally have visited many sacred places around the world, and I know very well the healing power of the water, respected by the people of those lands. A respect for the water that has stood the test of time for centuries.

When I went to another shamanic retreat in Mount Shasta years ago, one of the practices involved sitting in silence by the water. There was a creek nearby. The shaman said, **"The sound of the water beautifies the soul."** I will never forget this quote. This encapsulates quite poetically the wondrous effects of water as it uplifts our frequency.

One frequency I would love to mention is the Schumann resonance that was named after the physicist who, in 1956, published the Earth Resonance Study. Again, this fact has been also known by Native peoples from around the world for ages. It was only a discovery for the Westerners who did not grow up in cultures where a loving partnership with the Earth was second nature. The Earth, our beautiful planet, is a living, breathing being with its own heartbeat that beats at the frequency of 7.83 Hz. Not only that, our frequency and the Earth frequency are one. **Like human hearts and animal hearts,**

Earth's heart is an electromagnetic field, and we are connected to it whether we realize it or not.

Have you ever visited an ancient sacred site? Perhaps there are rocks where a sacred building once stood. Perhaps it was a megalithic site, a pyramid, a place of reverence for those who lived thousands of years ago, before the concept of church was ever introduced to the human psyche. Have you felt the Earth's frequency at a specific location? Has it given you an impression of peace, or oneness? Maybe like the feeling of perfect serenity in the early hours of the morning before the world wakes up when everything seems to be in complete harmony? Or the feeling of being in nature where no other people are around, and there is a clear sense of being connected to it all, a sense of belonging not felt in the city?

There is a certain quality these ancient places emanate. It is a frequency felt more strongly there than anywhere else. These sacred places were special locations where ancient people loved the Earth and where the heartbeat of the Earth can still be felt more strongly. As we continue to learn more about frequencies, I would love to make it clear that even our planet carries its signature frequency of love, and we can sense it when we visit nature in its most pristine form. Love is truly a force of nature, and it is not exclusive to humans. **When we learn to feel the different frequencies within us and around us, we can understand that Einstein was absolutely correct: Everything is energy.**

I consider the following story quite humorous. Every time I remember this moment, it does make me laugh. Animals did teach me a lesson. Here we go.

BIRDS IN THE HIMALAYAS

Before 2020, I had the opportunity to visit the North of India where the Dalai Lama lives. I was so excited to make my way to this very sacred part of this incredible subcontinent full of ancient wisdom and mystery.

I was in my humble hotel out in the mountains meditating by myself, enjoying the sunrise, looking at the marvelous natural beauty of this space. There were no other people around, but I did have an entire flock of birds perched on a fence near me lined up one next to the other. I meditate every day, but this was my first time that these many birds chose to join me in meditation.

I reveled in the sacredness of that moment. There I was taking in this Himalayan air, breathing it deeply in my lungs, recharging my body and my spirit. I was beyond ecstatic. The sun arose behind the majestic mountains, and the rays of light started to permeate the place with a soft luminosity. I was transfixed in my meditation. The birds were all there with me, still, just like I was.

I did not think much of their presence then because I was so in awe admiring the sacredness I could feel coming from those mountains. But then, as I came back from my meditative state, I noticed not one bird had left; in fact, more birds had come. There were also birds on the ground at the bottom of the fence. My human mind produced a silly thought: *Perhaps they are here waiting for my breakfast to arrive.* I imagined how sweet it would be to share my breakfast with them.

A person came with a platter and placed my breakfast on a small concrete table near where I was sitting. Still, just me. I was one with the majestic beauty of this place with no other humans around.

As I proceeded to take my first bite, every single bird flew away and did not come back!

WHAT I LEARNED FROM THIS STORY

The birds were there to bask in the beautiful frequency of the peace of my meditation. They were active participants of a sacred moment of communing with nature, with the mountains, with the sunrise. It was such a moment of complete reverence for creation. My human thought of waiting for my food was such an insult to them. They taught me a lesson by departing all at once when the food appeared. It was the frequency of peace they wanted to partake in, not my food. I learned my lesson.

In summary, we are not our stories. We are not our thoughts. We are unconditional love—the energy that makes our hearts beat. It is the energy we transmit all around us when we are in a state of harmonious presence. **Our heart is our compass for navigating life through the emotional responses we have to our life events**. When we are out of balance, our emotions are lower, transmitting lower frequencies that affect us and those around us. When we take ownership of our emotions and find ways to bring ourselves back to harmony, we live a happier and much healthier life and all those who cross paths with us benefit from it too.

One of my favorite quotes of all time because of how profound this truth is, comes from Mahatma Gandhi who said, "Be the change you want to see in the world." For me, that starts precisely with carrying a happier frequency because I personally would love to see a happier world.

I hope the stories of the slug, the salamanders, the hummingbirds, and the little birds in the Himalayas give us a notion of how the world does, in fact, respond to the frequency we carry in our hearts. If we ever need to know what frequency we carry, all we need to do is ask the question: What emotion am I feeling right now? If it is not love, peace, joy, or harmony, then we can work on finding our way back to love and recalibrate. After all, that is why we are here: to be happy! Let's start today, building a practice of happiness. It is one of our life's missions.

Next, I would love to share what the animals have taught me about unconditional love. After all, I did not arrive at these conclusions by studying books alone, but by studying life through the eyes of innocent perception, seeing the world through the hearts of the animals around me. They are true teachers of love. They have been the best mentors for me. Love is the force that makes the world go round and round—the love of life, the love of self, the love of presence. Simply love.

PART 3
UNCONDITIONAL LOVE

Based on my experience as an animal energy healing practitioner, I have learned many of the ways in which unconditional loving energy works. I have witnessed how bodies, situations, and perspectives change when infused with this divine frequency. In this chapter, I present my learnings from seeing it in action as well as sharing more stories of animals and how they heal us with their love.

Animal companions teach us how to be present in the moment, to trust, to open our hearts to infinite possibilities of love, to care about another selflessly. They are the best examples of living life with joy in the present moment. ***La joie de vivre.*** Those of us who have shared life with an animal by our side know this to be true. Animals who share childhood moments with us are there when we experience the most important milestones in our early life like starting school, graduating, getting our hearts broken for the first time, just to name a few. Later in our life, they are by our side as we hit adult milestones like starting a family, getting our first job, vacationing, moving to a new city or a new country, or simply being that wagging tail greeting us with excitement when we come home. **Animals have that undeniable power of connecting with our hearts instantly and uplifting our energy. This is the superpower of unconditional love.**

Animal companions are, in fact, the gateway to our heart—to the dimension of unconditional love where life is blissful right here, right now. Animals have great wisdom in them. They live in the moment, and they teach us to do the same every minute we spend in their presence. Their hearts are constantly vibrating to the frequency of unconditional love, and we do not need to measure the hertz range of their frequency to feel its benefits. Our hearts melt in their presence. Animals are indeed extraordinary teachers who give us an education on emotions and their frequencies of love, peace, joy, playfulness, calmness, and tranquility; animals transmit these frequencies when they are by our side feeling safe and cherished.

Animals have the ability to bring us back to a place of loving presence in our hearts regardless of the life events we are going through. A cat's purring has a frequency range of up to 150 Hz. If they sense our frequency is in the range of 150 Hz or below, in other words feelings of shame, guilt, and fear, our cats will instinctively come to us and purr on our chest to recalibrate our frequency. Similarly, dogs work on rebalancing our frequency. When we pet a dog and pass our hands through their fur, our heart rate variability (HRV) changes. This loving touch brings our frequency to a more relaxed and calmer range. No wonder so many of us benefit from the therapeutic effects of their presence and have begun to recognize them as our therapy and emotional companions.

All animals have an innate ability to rebalance us to a more relaxed state of being. This state of being gets activated through the frequency of our hearts, which in medical terms, can be measured through HRV. The higher the HRV, the calmer we are. The calmer we are, the more

PART 3: UNCONDITIONAL LOVE

balanced we feel. The more balanced we feel, the more pleasant our emotions are. The more pleasant our emotions are, the happier we are.

THE WATCHMAN AND BOBBY

I recently visited Scotland for my third time. This trip, I took extra time to visit the Greyfriars Kirkyard in Edinburgh where Bobby is buried. This beautiful story of unconditional love will warm your heart. In 1850, a night watchman of Edinburgh decided to accept a puppy given by a kind person from the community. He was not exactly looking to have a dog but something in his heart told him to accept this gift. Soon the puppy and he became inseparable and would do the rounds together in the city at night. The city people began to warm up to this duo who together worked hard at keeping the city safe. One sad day, the watchman contracted tuberculosis and died. In front of his beloved pup, he was put to rest in the Greyfriars Kirkyard. Once the burial was complete, Bobby did not move from the grave. Day after day he would stay by the grave waiting for his human to come out again. His human never did. Dogs were not allowed in cemeteries and the city tried to evict him many times, but he would always go back to his human's grave to wait for him. The only time he would leave the graveside was when the cannon in the city would announce 1:00 p.m., and he would run to the pub where he and his human used to have their meals together. There, a friend of the departed watchman had a meal for Bobby. Every single day he came and ate, then immediately after went back to the grave.

After nine years, the city passed an ordinance that any unregistered dog would be eliminated from the city grounds. To ensure Bobby would be saved, the pub's owner paid Bobby's registration fee, put a collar on him to make him legal and Bobby lived another four years in the cemetery. It was at the age of sixteen when he was finally reunited with his beloved human. He is buried at the entrance of the cemetery.

He is a beloved figure in Scottish history and has stolen the hearts of Edinburgh residents. The city erected a beautiful statue and fountain right outside the entrance of the cemetery a year after his death. There is also a prominent celebration of Bobby at the entrance of the cemetery with flowers and a plaque honoring the unconditional love he demonstrated for his beloved human.

There is a pub called Greyfriars Bobby, situated between Bobby's statue and the commemorative plaque at the entrance of Greyfriars Kirkyard, which was established twenty-one years after Bobby's death. Tourists and locals place sticks at the foot of the plaque in the cemetery as a present to Bobby so he can play with his sticks in the afterlife.

If you are ever in Edinburgh, I highly recommend visiting Bobby there. This real story of unconditional love will open your heart to the infinite power of love. There is an incredible number of stories of animals' unconditional love. I invite you to pay attention. They are indeed all around us—not always marked with a plaque or a statue, but they are there! Whether stories of animals loving humans or animal species loving other animal species, their unconditional love is immeasurably sublime. They are teaching us how to love unconditionally and without labels.

I would like to offer a very simple blessing to us all as we embark into the animal stories that have filled my heart with so much love all my life.

PART 3: UNCONDITIONAL LOVE

May this book be a nourishment for our souls.

May this book bring a fresh, new perspective to appreciate, and may we be grateful for the learnings of our past traumas and wounds.

May it also be an invitation to celebrate the extraordinary uniqueness that we bring to the world by being this wonderfully "flawed" beautiful us that we are!

May we celebrate the one-of-a-kind being that we are because indeed there is nobody like us in the entire world!

And may this book reconnect us to our true essence: LOVE.

—Stephanie

Animals have been teaching me something precious all my life: How to hold the frequency of unconditional love. It is an ineffable feeling. It is a truly divine experience. Animals have transformed my ordinary life into an extraordinarily sublime one. I am sharing this wisdom that has filled my soul with so much joy and peace. I hope this book brings us the keys we were looking for to open the door to our own personal happiness like animals did for me.

Life is a journey that ebbs and flows; the river of life is a constant enigmatic flow of change. There are mountains to climb and detours that bring us unexpected joys as well as unexpected sorrows. There are devastating events that build our resilience and inner strength. It surprises us! Life has it all. It shapes us, forms us, brings us to our knees, and it also picks us up. Rich with experiences, it is an overflowing cornucopia of emotions, feelings, thoughts and everything in between.

May this book help us get started in demystifying our own life events. As we extract the wisdom from these events, we will also bring extraordinary joy into every moment of our daily life regardless of where in our journey we are or what is happening around us.

HOW DID I START MY JOURNEY?

Ever since I can remember (around five years old is my earliest animal memory), I have been fascinated by animals, not because I wanted to study them scientifically, I wanted to connect with them. Animals' eyes spoke to me. I saw a divine power in their eyes as if they were angels on Earth in different colors, shapes, and forms. I have always felt so loved in their presence, like all was good in the world if I was next to an animal. Dogs, cats, birds, frogs, chickens, cows, fish, rabbits, horses, donkeys… All animals are fascinating. I absolutely love how they make me feel in their presence. It is quite literally the feeling of being loved by God by simply looking into their eyes.

Some of us connect with a higher power when we admire a beautiful sunset that brings peace to our hearts. Or the sense of power as we arrive at the summit of a mountain and admire the view from above. Perhaps it's our fascination for birds or flowers and their infinite diversity of colors, shapes, sizes, and aromas. Or maybe it's even the high we feel when running a marathon and tapping into that sense of invincibility within us. All these are examples of our connecting with that higher power within us, in our hearts: **Unconditional love, or higher power is, in fact, our superpower.**

Animals are my connection to a higher power. Their eyes are the windows, not just to their souls, but also to the physical representation of the higher power of love that some of us call God or Source. What an absolute miracle it is to see the multiple shapes, forms, and faces of that higher power, omnipresent in our life journey. The same divine essence is also within us. It is what fascinated me all my childhood.

However, it did not take me long to realize that not everybody saw animals the way I did.

Most people had divided animals into two very distinct categories: animals worthy of our love (dogs and cats for example) and animals for exploitation, seen merely as objects of a cruel food supply system.

Seeing this disparity as a kid was heartbreaking. I wanted to be a voice for the animals and help people open their eyes to see what I could see. But as a kid, of course, I was ignored and often dismissed. So, I made it a mission to help stray dogs, to give them love and food. I took many to the vet to get care after some heartless, reckless driver caused them harm without any regret. Perhaps after reading these animal stories, we can all see animals under a different light. Perhaps we can all hear the calling to help those animals who are still being victimized by our food supply, medical, and commercial structures.

My grandma's menagerie were my beloved animal companions; I never saw them as being lesser beings than humans. In fact, in my eyes, they were in a *higher* category than humans because unlike us, animals love unconditionally regardless of what we do, what we wear, what car we drive, what job we have, how we look, or how our day has been. They just love us for the light we have within. Not all humans can do the same. We certainly can learn from them how to love without judgments, without labels.

As a teenager, veterinary medicine was the only path I knew to helping animals. But after befriending our neighborhood vet, I soon realized, it would break my heart on a daily basis when I saw firsthand how many animals were euthanized. This act had become mechanical and deprived of sensitivity for someone who does it on a regular basis. At that point in my life, I could not envision myself having the ability to euthanize animals and keep it together. Performing this act would have made me incredibly unhappy. I decided to release my lifelong dream of helping animals as a veterinary professional. Veterinary medicine was clearly not the path for me.

Decades later, I am reconnecting with my lifelong dream of being the voice of the animals and helping them through my energy healing practice. I feel like my heart bursts with joy every time I stop and think, *I am helping animals everyday now*. Not only that, but I am no longer the kid who is dismissed when she tries to educate humans on how special and miraculous animals are. Now, as an adult I am capable of articulating my feelings more clearly so the message can be understood. I am now fulfilling my desire of being that voice of the animals. Finally!

Spikey is my animal energy healing mentor. Many of us know how special the bond is with an animal companion in our life. We know how they can shower us with their loving energy every day. I dabbled in the Animal Healing Practice thanks to him. My great friend Barbara Beach was about to teach a Reiki training and asked me if I was interested in learning it. At that time, I had not been exposed to Reiki teachings to know exactly what it was. I had received Reiki during a chiropractor session and the sense of well-being I felt lasted for over two weeks. I was in such a state of joyful harmony with the world that my physical, mental, and emotional bodies all felt in perfect balance. I don't remember ever feeling like that before. It was as if everything was good in the world, my world. I realized I could learn Reiki and repeat this experience, so I was all in. That is where my journey began.

In order to move from the initial level of Reiki to the next, I had to put in hours of practice at each level. My daughter was not always a willing subject to my practice, but Spikey always was. How did I know he was willing? Because every single time I sat on the couch ready to initiate a session, without being called, he would immediately jump on the couch right next to me indicating, *I am ready; let's begin.*

As I practiced with him, I noticed how his body started to relax. His muscles twitched as if releasing tension and stiffness. His body softened. I would see him fall into a very deep sleep with his entire body stretched out to occupy the whole space. It was a very distinct posture quite different from his typical sleeping one. I realized he was truly taking in all the energy I transmitted, and his physical body really enjoyed it.

What were the immediate effects of Reiki on Spikey? Besides having a very positive demeanor, which he had always had anyway, his chronic ear allergies and infections, which he had battled since he adopted us, started to subside. I struggled to find a permanent solution to his very sensitive ears. The vet and I had tried different diets, removing harsh chemicals from the house, and more. The last resort, of course, was considering ongoing medication. But I just did not want to give him medication for allergies that, over time, would damage his liver. My Reiki healing practice paired with a more wholesome diet was able to finally take care of his chronic ear infections for good.

This is when I realized I could bring energy healing services to the animals. In return, they shared their wisdom with me.

Traditional Reiki was my starting point. I continued with Shelter Animal Reiki and started volunteering regularly in farm animal sanctuaries. Most recently I've learned the modalities of Pendragon Reiki and Dragon Empowerment Reiki. All four modalities are rooted in the healing frequency of unconditional love, and each has a distinct energetic quality. One is more earthy, one is more peaceful, one is more loving, and one is more nurturing. I feel the energy that comes through is a little different when connecting with each of these modalities. Every person may feel a different quality. It is not always the same for everyone. They all are healing, loving energies that transmit soft and gentle healing power. The intensities may also vary depending on the animal and what is needed in the moment. Energy flow varies from animal to animal and from day to day.

Unconditional love—being a frequency that resonates at a higher level than dis-ease—pushes away energetic blockages which cause the body to not be in its optimal state of homeostasis. That higher frequency is energy healing. It is unconditional love at work. It is magnificent, and it is quite literally nirvana—a pure state of bliss. No human-made artifact or product can reproduce the sublime feeling of the unconditional love frequency. Its power is limitless. **We all have it in us, and we can harness it, amplify it, expand it, and share it with others**. This is energy healing.

I appreciate your being here. Thank you for wanting to learn about what animals have to say about unconditional love, about happiness, about enlightenment. Thank you for being a human with an open heart who appreciates the sublime quality of unconditional love that animals exude with their mere presence. You are the reason I wrote this book!

HOW DO ANIMALS RESPOND TO ENERGY?

We discussed earlier about how I came to love animals so much. But who are they and what is our relationship to them? This is my definition of animals based on my personal experience, not based on textbook learning.

Animals are highly evolved energetic creatures, able to see energies our human eye cannot perceive.

They have the ability to identify multiple levels of frequencies in a much wider spectrum than humans can.

They communicate through these highways of higher energy frequencies we have yet to deeply understand and utilize for better and clearer communication.

Animals use the geomagnetic fields of the Earth to navigate through space, through seasons, through air, earth, and water. This is an ability that only those very close to the Earth and the elements are able to replicate, such as all Indigenous tribes all over our planet.

Animals have a primal sense of survival, and yet, they have an incredible sense of empathy toward other species. This is something humans who are disconnected from the Earth do not easily do. We do not show empathy to our own species most of the time, except to those in our close circle of loved ones. Fortunately, I see that we are learning how to be more empathic.

Animals have deep feelings. They experience fear, love, and concern for others, and they instinctively sound the alarm to raise awareness of danger when predators approach. They also communicate the presence of food or shelter. They mourn and grieve intensely the loss of their partners, offspring, and elders.

Animals can read the energy of the elements easily and know where to go and when to stay to keep safe and protected. They navigate the frequencies of the elements with dexterity, while most humans can't do it on their own and rely heavily on Wi-Fi, apps, or a plethora of instruments and gadgets.

Of these qualities, what I particularly admire most about animals is their incredible open hearts; it is their superpower. Animals can read our hearts' energy like we are an open book. They do it so easily because their hearts are intrinsically open already. They are not fearful of humans unless humans have given them a reason to be. They hold the frequency of unconditional love with ease and grace. **Animals reflect to us so wonderfully well the energy we shine on them**. They are not just our gateway to a higher power, but they are also mirrors. A fearful human will encounter a fearful animal. A loving human will encounter a loving animal. Of course there are times when other humans have caused trauma and fear to animals before we arrive so there is damage to be repaired and this is where energy healing comes into play.

WHO ARE HUMANS?

I believe the Hawaiians describe this relationship between humans and animals very well with the word *kahu*. Kahu is someone who acts as the guardian, the protector. We cherish animals; we safeguard them. We live on this Earth along with them. We honor their presence because they, like us, carry that divine essence in them. They are not lesser beings, they are our equals in many ways, but they are higher evolved beings in many other ways. We are here to live with them, respect them, learn from them, and allow them to teach us to exist in a way that is in harmony with creation. There is plenty we can learn from Indigenous cultures, their deep respect for animals, and how they value and honor their lives.

We as humans have the power to create and to destroy. A respectful human will choose to create, to live in harmony, and to honor life. **Animals can teach us how to use our power responsibly** by coexisting in a loving and harmonious manner with other beings who do not speak the human language but connect with us through the frequency of an open heart.

It is not complicated.

We make it complicated when we put labels on how we are to behave with some animals but not with others. There are no labels. We as humans owe it to ourselves to open our hearts to this truth so we can learn what living in the frequency of unconditional love is all about. We will very quickly realize this is the way to live, the *only* way that will allow us to thrive. This is the way, and **animals are our wayshowers, our unconditional love teachers**.

Now that we understand these fundamental concepts about animals, energy, and the healing power of energy, let's get started with a few of my stories that highlight how unconditional love brings change in our lives, big and small, expected and unexpected. The magic lies in having an open heart and an open mind and letting the energy rebalance what needs to be rebalanced without trying to force a specific result. I particularly love the little things the most, because they happen daily and are constant reminders of how we create our life based on the energy we emit and transmit.

My hope is that these animal stories transcend the confines of the written word to open our hearts to our infinite inner power and inner light like they did with mine. In my classes, I bring a box of tissues for my students because when the heart opens, the tears flow. I recommend having some nearby just in case these stories touch your heart in a similar way. I hope these stories paint the picture of how everything is possible when we are vibrating with the energy of love.

MY FIRST RAINBOW BRIDGE EXPERIENCE

Early in my practice, I had been very focused on being an energy healing practitioner who brought physical, emotional, mental, and energetic well-being to all animals. However, I was facing the transition of a beloved dog I used to pet sit regularly. Bidu and Spikey were best buds. They spent every weekend together. But they had several years of age difference. Bidu was quickly approaching the moment when he would cross the rainbow bridge and none of us, his family or us, were ready for that.

This is when I discovered how the frequency of unconditional love can bring peace in a moment of pure agonizing despair. As animal lovers, the bond we have with our animal companions does not compare to any other bond we create during our lives. How can we ever be ready to say goodbye? Even if we are ready, how can we do it guilt-free? How can we do it with a peaceful heart? It is never ever easy. This was an incredible revelation. **The energy of love can bring a sense of tranquil acceptance in the moment of a heartbreaking departure.**

One day, my friends called in tears and said, "Stephanie, it is time; we need to take Bidu to the vet to be put to sleep, and we don't know if we are emotionally strong enough to go." I asked to please let me go with them. There I was at the vet's office with my friends and Bidu, facing the exact reason I did not think I could go into veterinary school. How could I stay strong in this moment? I knew transitioning to the other side is not the end, it is a transition, and the animal still lives in another form—one of pure loving energy. The difference is the body no longer contains their energy. It is wonderful to know they, just like humans, do not cease to exist.

I kept this knowledge in my heart as they injected the solution into Bidu's veins in front of the heavy hearts of my two friends and me. The vet left the room and allowed us to have our final moments with him alone. I helped them direct their attention not to the sadness of the separation but to the beauty of his life with them, how happy Bidu had been with them all these years, the peacefulness of his sleep, how happy he would be on the other side, pain-free, and how he would live in our hearts always. I helped them redirect their sorrow toward celebrating the joy he brought with his presence—the same joy that lives in our hearts for as long as we remember him. As we all focused on the feeling of celebration rather than sorrow, we were able to see him quickly and peacefully transition. He departed being celebrated and feeling deeply loved.

The vet walked in and said the process had been fast. Bidu's face looked so peaceful and none of us was sobbing. Sad yes, but not devastated. I realized how powerful the unconditional love frequency is. We were all able to keep it together and not fall into agonizing despair.

I knew then: I can do this because my heart did not break. The hearts of my friends were also comforted during this heartbreaking moment of goodbye.

As I write this story, I can feel the heaviness we felt as we went to the vet together. But at the same time, I also feel the lightness of heart as we knew he had transitioned peacefully and was no longer in pain, and I can tap into the feeling we all had of getting through it without falling apart. Of course, we were not joyful, but we had an inexplicable inner peace that left the vet's staff puzzled. The staff all looked quite dumbfounded when we did not come out of the room sobbing, which is typically what they are used to seeing.

WHAT I LEARNED FROM THE RAINBOW BRIDGE CROSSING

I knew right then I would be able to help many more animals transition peacefully and also help their humans navigate through this experience with a lighter heart. I feel so blessed to have the opportunity to work with this gift. I knew I wanted to teach others how they could do the same. My goal is for all animals to have animal healers around them. Always! This means, we need to grow in numbers. We must hold the loving frequency in our hearts for as long as we possibly can day after day so we can transmit love and peace to all those beautiful animals around us.

RED WING BLACK BIRD SONG

I find all sorts of animals to be marvels of creation. Birds are no exception. There was one particular bird song so distinctly unique and pleasant to my ears, I had come to intently listen for it during my walks with Spikey. I am sure by now you have noticed a theme with my lifestyle. Marvelous experiences do happen regularly when I go out for walks in nature. I make it a point to do this daily for wondrous things to occur. I invite synchronicities in with open heart and mind.

Endless possibilities lead to sublime experiences in the two to three mile radius of my home.

Over the course of many walks, I encountered this beautifully enchanting song of the red wing black bird. I would hear it, locate where it was coming from, and pause to enjoy the sound. I was fortunate to find this bird very often during my walks. It brought so much joy and peace to my heart. I never knew I would be so mesmerized by this one bird song. Of all the birds, this song has the power to stop me in my tracks and invite me to enjoy its unique beauty—an invitation I never refuse.

One day turned out to be a quite unique experience. I was about to finish my three-mile walk and had not encountered the song of my beloved red wing black bird when suddenly at a far distance where I had not heard it before, the bird made an audible appearance, although I was still unable to see exactly where it was coming from.

To my surprise, the bird flew directly toward me and perched on a power line a few feet directly above me. He sang and sang and sang. I had the distinct feeling the bird had literally come for a little private concert. I felt so very special he had intentionally done this for me.

Minutes went by, and I could have stood there quite possibly a solid ten minutes, but Spikey was ready to keep going. I very gratefully said goodbye to the bird who left the moment I walked away.

It was then that I knew without a shred of doubt, that the bird had specifically come to sing to me and was willing to stay for as long as I wanted to listen. What a heartwarming experience that was. Some people may call this a coincidence; I call it synchronicity. The difference? Coincidence means these events are random in nature. Synchronicities are intentional; there is nothing random about them.

Next time we encounter an animal, let's not take crossing paths for granted. Let's pause for a moment to notice them and pay attention to where they came from. What was in our thoughts and heart the moment they showed up? Soon we will discover they very likely had a message for us that only we would know. They can sense our energy, and they respond to it in the same way this amazing red wing black bird came to me and sang because he knew I had a deep desire in that moment to listen to his song.

WHAT I LEARNED FROM THE RED WING BLACK BIRD

Next time we see a bird that speaks to us in a special way, perhaps consider taking a pause and connecting. It is in the realm of infinite possibilities that we will receive a special message. We will never know unless we try. **No animal ever crosses our paths by chance**. It is a synchronous event not to take for granted.

SENIOR DOG MISSING!

I was relaxing at home during my Christmas staycation one year when I got this text from someone. *Could you help me communicate with my senior dog?*

This dog had gone missing overnight in Oregon wine country and he needed his medication. His human explained he was an older dog and would have lots of difficulty finding his way back home due to early dementia. I responded via text, *I am happy to help and will do my very best, but I cannot give any guarantees because missing animals are not my specialty.*

Animals are not looking at street signs, house numbers, or the types of coordinates we use to identify an address. They are animals, connected to the Earth, and their sense of location is very different from ours. This is why it is a bit more difficult but not impossible to get precise information from an animal.

I went ahead and connected. I saw the dog on the side of the road surrounded by open fields with a cloudy sky. He was walking but with no clear direction as to where to go. There were no houses around, just open fields by the road where he was. The dog felt to me like he was tired, confused, and lost.

I suggested the dog's mom imagine she was a beacon of light, pouring the love she has for her dog out in this light. Her dog could then see it wherever he was and use it to find his way back home.

She followed my instructions and the next morning as early as 6:00 a.m. I got her text indicating her dog had made his way back home. Her poor dog must have walked all night. Animals see the light spectrum in ways the human eye cannot. It was the love energy frequency she was broadcasting to him that showed him the way home. I did not find the dog, rather the dog found his human. I simply provided instructions to facilitate the safe return home.

WHAT THIS SENIOR DOG TAUGHT ME

We are more powerful than we think. The next time we are in a situation that brings us anxiety, let's consider the possibility of stopping those incessant thoughts of worry and remember this story. Focusing on a positive result can bring about the outcome we wish. Focusing energy on what we want instead of what we are worried about is the lesson here.

MAHANA, MY LITTLE FRIEND

This awesome Boston terrier Mahana is a fantastic dog. She is the mentor of a dear friend of mine, a special dog who has a mission to help, guide, and assist my friend in her spiritual practice, which she does remarkably well.

Over the years, her tiny physical body has started to show signs of aging which of course is never easy for the loving human mom. My friend reached out to me one day asking for my help. She can connect with her own dog of course but her emotions and worries were getting in the way and clouding her understanding of what was going on with Mahana's health. She worried that cancer had come back and needed a clear answer so she would know if it was right to subject her beloved Mahana to all the testing this would entail.

I connected with her and got a very direct message that it was *not* cancer. She did not go into more detail than that. It was not difficult to believe other sorts of masses could appear in her body unrelated to cancer. **Energy trapped in the body will eventually manifest as some type of health issue**—true for humans too. *The Emotion Code* by Dr. Bradley Nelson explains this in detail. If you have heard that our bodies keep the score of all we go through emotionally, you can understand the premise of *The Emotion Code* book. It decodes and shows how different emotions translate into different physical ailments; for example, grief can manifest in heart problems, anxiety can manifest in digestion problems, and insecurity can manifest in lower back problems just to name a few.

I relayed the information to my friend, and she was deeply relieved to hear it was not cancer. Nobody wants to subject their dog to cancer surgery and treatment. It is incredibly stressful emotionally and financially. I told my friend what I tell everyone: Use this information to go to the vet informed. It takes a lot of the agonizing guessing out of the equation. The human and the vet can narrow down the issue and go to treatment faster and more easily.

WHAT I LEARNED FROM THIS STORY

Animal companions are always here to mirror back to us what is going on. Let's always pay attention to what physical signs they show, because chances are, they are showing us where to pay attention in our own body. Mahana was in fact mirroring my friend as a loving reminder to take care of herself.

LUNA, MY BEARDED DRAGON

This story is about my own reptile animal companion. It is a short and sweet story but so worth mentioning because I know many of us can relate to this.

A bearded dragon's constipation can be a sign of serious health problems. I knew about this, so I started getting very worried shortly after she was adopted, when she was not doing her business.

I worried she may become septic if she did not go soon. I was, after all, a new reptile mom and was learning how to take care of her the best way I could.

Then one night I dreamed that she had finally gone and done her business, and in my dream, I was so relieved that she was OK and would no longer have to worry about her health.

When I woke up the next day, I got up, got ready, did all the things I needed to do to get myself to work on time and did not remember my dream. But as I came back home that day, I saw Luna had finally gone. At that moment, I saw my dream as a flashback in my mind, which is when I realized my bearded dragon had talked to me in my dream to let me know not to worry, that it would happen.

WHAT I LEARNED FROM LUNA

Animals may communicate with us through our dreams. Journaling about our dreams allows us to remember those messages more consistently.

Imagine having an ongoing communication with your animal companion by paying attention to your dreams!

PART 3: UNCONDITIONAL LOVE

CHARLENE, MY CHILDHOOD PARROT

I grew up in one of the beautiful tropical paradises on Earth, Costa Rica. One day when I was about ten, I was gifted a small, green parrot. I was so happy! Finally, I got to have my very own animal companion. I named her Charlene after the character of a TV show I was watching at the time.

Charlene slept in her cage at night but the rest of the day she had complete freedom to fly anywhere in the house. Most of the time she chose to be on my shoulder and be with me as I did my homework and went around the house completing activities and chores. She would eat off my plate, play with my earrings, and fall asleep with me as I watched TV. We were bonded. We were inseparable.

However, one day, as I had put her in the bathroom to keep her safe from my grandma's cat, she fell in the toilet and drowned. My heart was broken. I have no words to describe how devastated I felt. She was my only animal companion. We did everything together and due to my childish ignorance on proper ways to keep her safe, I had been the cause of her demise. I felt guilty and depressed.

I remember her, and I always think of her as the animal companion that brought so much joy in a time when I did not receive much love from the humans in my life other than my grandma.

Fast forward to a few decades later: I was participating in a gallery reading at the Oregon Ghost Conference. There I was surrounded by over one hundred people. Suddenly, the psychic who was doing the readings said he could see a bird flying around the room. I did not think much of it because I had lost Charlene so many years before that I could not imagine it would be her.

As the physic kept providing details about how she looked and how she died, I knew he was speaking to me. I raised my hand and acknowledged that yes, I did have a parrot as a kid and yes, she had a very sudden death for which to this day I still feel guilty about. The psychic said Charlene wanted to say how sorry she was for leaving me so abruptly. She had cherished the bond we had and loved me very much. She was sad to see me grieve for her for so long. As the intuitive delivered this message, I had tears in my eyes and could not utter a word. After all these years, here she was telling me how sorry she was for leaving. What a gift that was to close my childhood wound.

WHAT I LEARNED FROM CHARLENE

When our beloved animals pass away, they are still with us; they are just in energy form. If we are thinking of them, chances are they are thinking about us too. We receive their telepathic telegram, and they receive ours. Knowing this, we can choose at any time to communicate with them as if they are still here, because in an energetic form, they actually are.

DRAGONFLIES

Recently I obtained Levels 1 and 2 of two additional types of Dragon Reiki, Pendragon Reiki and Dragon Empowerment Reiki. (I continuously expand my practice and incorporate different modalities.)

As I connected with the angelic and quite powerful dragon energy, I started to consistently encounter dragonflies everywhere. It was so miraculous to witness because I hadn't remembered seeing dragonflies in years. There they were, suddenly, present around me wherever I went.

I know quite well these are synchronicities with a message directed to me. The dragon energy I was incorporating in my practice was making its presence known in the physical realm.

WHAT I LEARNED FROM THIS

Let's pay attention to the little creatures. They too give us messages and they are all around us. What messages do they have for us today or tomorrow? These dragonflies were acknowledging the spiritual work I was doing then and made themselves quite visible to me. It was as if to say, "We see you."

SPIKEY'S NOT EATING

I was away on a trip and my friend was taking care of Spikey. She told me she was worried he looked sad, and she conveyed that he was not eating. She asked if she should take him to the vet.

I was not going to be home for another week or so. I connected with him remotely to ask what was wrong and how I could help. Spikey immediately showed me an image of him gnawing at a bone I had brought to him from the farmers' market. I got the clear answer from Spikey himself. The bone had broken a tooth, and he was in pain and could not chew his food. I asked my friend to give him bland food he would not have to chew, and said I would take him to the vet to get his teeth examined since this was very much the reason he was refusing to eat.

I made the appointment with the vet from abroad and when I got back home, I took him to get examined and the vet corroborated the message Spikey gave me. She examined his teeth and found the damaged tooth that had to be removed.

Fortunately, once the tooth was extracted, Spikey resumed his normal eating routine, and I never bought him a bone ever again. Other chewable healthy treats yes, but never a bone.

WHAT I LEARNED FROM THIS STORY

When we do not know what is going on with our beloved animals, we need to ask them. With an open heart and an open mind, listen. They will give us an answer. It can come in a myriad of ways: an image, a hunch, a certainty of what it is. Just keeping an open mind will facilitate the communication. I so appreciate knowing this open channel of communication exists, and I do ask questions all the time. Maybe not daily but every time I feel confused or at a loss, I remember to ask. So can all of us.

DOG WITH EPILEPSY

Many times, I get called to figure out how to help a case that seems very confusing. The human reaching out on behalf of their beloved animal companion is at a loss as to what is happening. This was the case with a dog who was two or three years old and had recently developed a strange behavior. He was being crate-trained at night, which was when he began having seizures. They reached out to inquire what was going on.

I connected with the dog and examined his energetic field quite thoroughly to identify where this was coming from. Could it be chemicals in the house, highly toxic chemicals in the lawn, or toxic food he had ingested by accident? There was also the possibility of a genetic issue starting to manifest in his brain such as epilepsy. I did not know what it was, and I worked on not setting any expectations as to what it might be. I did the energetic scan with a very open mind and a chart of the anatomy of a dog so I would be able to identify the organ or organs where the energetic imbalance was occurring. I found it in a specific part of his brain.

When I relayed the information to his human, he explained to me his own history. When he was a kid, he had had brain cancer precisely on the part of the brain I had just mentioned. Was this a coincidence? I don't believe in coincidences. I believe in synchronicities, and they all have messages.

Next, the human proceeded to inquire with the vet if there was, in fact, treatment for what he believed was the cause of the seizures and his dog's change of behavior. The impossible vet bill made his treatment and surgery a financial challenge that he was not able to overcome. Based on the vet's advice that seizures were bound to get worse over time, he decided in the best interest of his animal companion that putting him to sleep was the most loving thing he could do for him.

As I go into energy healing sessions, I always go with the intention of being of service. I do not have an agenda of how things need to turn out. I am happy to be there and know that whatever happens is happening for the highest and greatest good of all involved. I do know that death is only a transition to another world. It is not the end of a beloved being. Is this dog better there than here based on these circumstances? The dog must decide for himself. His human needs to follow his intuition to pick up on the subtle messages his dog is sending him.

I do not know if the surgery and treatment and the many thousands of dollars would have changed the course of the type of brain cancer he had. What I do know is that this dog was very happy to have lived the life he had. He had lots of playtime and attention with his human. He had his undivided devotion every day. His life was better because of him. Whatever duration that life was, it had made his awesome puppy heart happy. In the end, isn't this what matters most? How much happiness are we able to bring to these beautiful animals?

WHAT I LEARNED FROM THIS STORY

My goal is to always be of service to the animals. Sometimes this means assisting them with their healing and sometimes with their transition across the rainbow bridge. In the end, the choice is not mine but theirs.

THE NOT-SO-SOCIAL COW

A cow was rescued from an abusive environment and brought to an Oregon farm animal sanctuary. This cow was not like the others in the sanctuary. She used her horns to push the other cows away and feed from the hay all by herself. The other cows learned to keep their distance from her. It was a behavior that none of the other cows exhibited. I was wondering: *What is making her feel so protective of her space and keeping everyone away?* Cows are herd animals and normally stick together. What happened? At the sanctuary, nobody knew the reason for this behavior.

I asked friends from my spiritual group if we could collectively connect with her and help her feel at ease in her new forever home. We soon discovered something that scientists have written about recently. Emotions from our parents are genetically stored in our DNA. The suffering our parents go through is stored in our cells as if we ourselves had gone through that suffering too. This is also true for animals, and it was certainly true for this cow. She was exhibiting behaviors that were the result of the trauma her mom had endured during her life. We must wonder: How do we heal from something we have not suffered from directly? I believe it to be in the same way we heal from all experiences in which we *have* been present.

We proceeded to send her love. Lots and lots of unconditional love. I use this word interchangeably with energy healing in this context. Pure love. Divine love. Unadulterated, no-hidden-agendas kind of love. Love that is there to be of service, no personal expectations. Just love.

Again, amazing things happened. This remote session of love done by my three friends and me, made a difference in how this cow was feeling around other cows. Her demeanor seemed to be more peaceful. She began to show a sense of ease.

This is an example of how unconditional love heals. It heals the emotional wounds, whether they are our own or our parents' or grandparents' wounds stored in our DNA, and it works the same way with animals. Energy healing provides that transformative loving power. It is amazing to see the results.

What truly melted my heart happened after this remote session, when I visited the sanctuary again. Muddy boots and dirty hands, I was in full-on cleaning mode at the barn. I made my way to see this cow and see how she was doing and how the interaction was going with the others. Typically, a very loving bull would be the one to notice me from across the field and come to warmly greet me and say thank you for being here. But to my surprise, something unique occurred. The cow we worked on remotely was the one who came from the opposite side of the field and very slowly and intentionally walked in a straight line directly toward me, locking eyes with mine every step of the way. I knew in that moment she had recognized me and knew I was part of the energy healing she had received. She came to thank me. Just like that. I was so moved that it made me tear up in gratitude that she had acknowledged my service to her.

It is nice when a human says thanks. But when an animal goes out of their way to show gratitude, there is something quite extraordinary that touches my heart every time.

WHAT I LEARNED FROM THIS SPECIAL COW

When we encounter an animal that has what we may call a less-than-desirable behavior, I encourage us all to remember that each animal has a story, and chances are, it's a traumatic one. They too need love to overcome their story. Showing consistent and unconditional love to the animal will help them heal from their trauma. As a result, their behavioral "issues" will slowly subside.

CROSSING THE RAINBOW, MULTIPLE STORIES

Out of all the stories I have been telling you in this compilation, the most heartwarming stories are the ones where the animals cross over. Here is why.

Death, even though it is not the end, is a change. It is the transition from one realm into another. We all know how we feel about change. Some of us get incredibly apprehensive, even fearful, and some of us take the sense of adventure with a peaceful heart. Animals are the same. Some may have a tinge of apprehension in letting go and others will be more peaceful about the moment. It all depends on the bonds with their humans and the sadness they know their humans will experience as a result of their passing. In all the cases where I had the opportunity to be present during their passing, I was blessed to help them feel more relaxed and able to ease into the moment. The outcome of this was beautiful as each passing was quick, peaceful, with minimal labored breathing, and reduced fear: A far less apprehensive letting go.

WHAT I HAVE REALIZED DURING THESE TRANSITIONS

Once we understand that death is not the end but a transition, being there for these animals as they go across the rainbow bridge is an honor we should not take lightly. The trust they have in us to usher them into the afterlife is one of the most heartwarming experiences I have been blessed to witness time and time again.

When we remove our feelings to bear witness to this transition to the other realm, we can start to comprehend what a miraculous thing this really is. Their lives transcend beyond the constructs of time and space. We are present as they cross this earthly portal. The key to end our suffering is to consider this: Can we remove our feelings and experience this moment with a curious mind and not a heavy heart? That is the question! The answer is yes! We certainly can! I could not go to vet school when I was younger because of the fear of repeated heartbreak. Fast forward to today and I have been of service to many animals and my heart is not broken. I hope this message brings hope because at one time or another, we all will face our beloved animal companions' crossing. How will we choose to show up in that moment? My hope is this: with a heart full of unconditional love that ushers them peacefully and lovingly to the other realm.

We have gone over multiple examples of how animals respond to our energy frequency. We have talked about how unconditional love is a superpower, received and emitted by our hearts. We have also covered how the essence of who we are lies in our hearts as well. The very big question we may be asking ourselves now is this: In a world of turmoil, chaos, loss, and pain, how can we ever uplift our spirits to consistently carry this higher unconditional love frequency? What steps can we take to cultivate this discipline of happiness? Wisdom is bliss as I mentioned earlier. In the next chapter, we will be extracting the wisdom shared by the animal stories and go over a list of simple steps. This practice will help recalibrate our superpower on a daily basis to create monumental transformation over time. Let's dive in!

PART 4
PRACTICING OPENING OUR HEARTS

Before we get into the steps that allow us to open our hearts and harness happiness, I would love to emphasize the importance of **always filling our cup before we help those we love**. It is simple, but not easy. It requires a diligent daily routine. The more love we hold in our hearts, the easier it is to see transformation in our lives and in the lives of our loved ones. We talk about unconditional love energy as a superpower. It is real. It is palpable. It is present in each and every one of us. All we need to do is harness it. The practices in this chapter will help us accomplish that!

In case you ever wonder if **unconditional love is a real force of nature**, I would love to share a fun fact about this power. Unconditional love can be seen through the third eye chakra. I see it in trees, in waterfalls, in the sky, and in the animals too. I see it in the rays of the sun. It is a subtle light with pastel-like rainbow colors like the one I see in my bearded dragon, Luna. It is soft, translucent, and delicate. Sometimes it is an arc-shaped rainbow like the ones we are all familiar with. Sometimes it is a wisp-like cloud. It does not have a solid shape or definition.

In fact, the next animal story is one of the most beautiful moments of a feline's unconditional love captured on my daughter's phone camera.

CLOVER AND ZEN, THE RAINBOW CATS

My daughter and her roommate had two female cats they had recently adopted a few months apart, Clover and Zen.

I remember connecting with my daughter's cat regularly to provide assistance since these two kitties chased each other constantly and my daughter was worried they were not getting along. Over time, their love for each other grew and I am sure they learned to get along on their own. Perhaps the energy healing I sent was just a little nudge that helped them go in the right direction, or perhaps they had loved each other all along and the energy healing just intensified this loving connection. The kitties will know the answer to this question.

One very ordinary day, the two kitties were lying in bed just a foot away from each other. The sun was shining through the window and they both were happily sunbathing. Cats absolutely love the cleansing rays of sunlight. It is not just the warmth it brings to their bodies, but it is also a recharging of their spirit. They are reenergized and recalibrated. This is what I have observed by watching cats bask in the sun.

My daughter was enjoying watching them and something told her to take a picture of them. The magic was captured in the picture: There was a rainbow connecting both kitties. The fun part of this is that the picture was taken indoors. A rainbow inside the house has no logical explanation for me, so what it represents is the unconditional love energy these two kitties feel for each other. The camera somehow had in fact captured this connection. I have shown this picture on multiple platforms. It is just magical. Some may believe it is photoshopped, and some believe it is AI, but some of us just know it is real, and there are no gimmicks involved.

Remember what I mentioned earlier about how special animals are? Well, in the picture, Clover is looking at the rainbow in awe. Animals can actually *see* love! Clover was seeing the love between her and Zen in that exact moment, and there is a picture which captured their loving energy. How amazing is that?

WHAT I LEARNED FROM THIS STORY

I learned that animals are experts when it comes to unconditional love. They are here in part to teach us to love unconditionally and with an open heart. If we can learn to emulate their unconditional love, we would be the best version of ourselves.

The question now is this: How do we even start opening our hearts? How can we shed years and years of shutting down and begin to open up again? I would like to share how it started for me.

Over two decades ago when I started meditating, I remember reading one of Deepak Chopra's books. This has stayed with me all these years. He said to spend at least ten minutes a day doing the things we love. What a revelation! Why did I not think of that myself? Why did someone have to give me permission to get away from my daily, professional, and parenthood duties and truly dedicate a moment to my own happiness? Not somebody else's but mine. I felt so good. I called it Me Time, and my daughter learned to respect her mom's Me Time each day. Fast forward to today and my entire day is based on Me Time, because I have developed a practice that allows me to insert joy in all I do all day long. I went from ten minutes a day to twenty-four hours a day in twenty years. I believe I took this learning to heart, and I am quite pleased with the results. My formula from twenty years ago which

I still feel stands true today is this: ten minutes of stillness daily plus ten minutes of joy daily equals consistent happiness.

I hope all of us, too, can give ourselves the permission to cultivate small happy moments that, over time, will create a happy life. I'll bet we can all remember when we were in school. We needed a signed paper from the school office if we needed to leave early, right? With the following small permission slip, we can make our personal Me Time official. By adding our signature, we will be creating a contract with ourselves to work on our happiness. We just need to add our name and sign the following two lines. Let's do it. Let's actually make this official. There is a legitimacy of our intention when we make the effort to have a tangible object that reflects what we intend to do next. I invite us all to go grab a piece of paper and write the following statement:

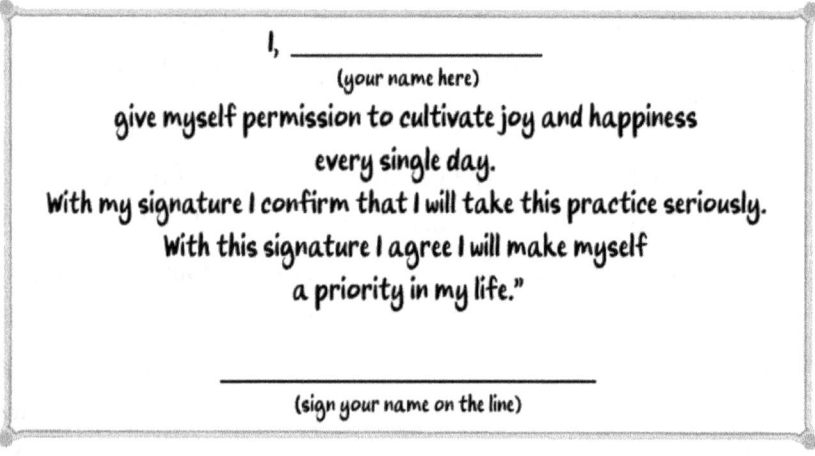

I, _____
(your name here)
give myself permission to cultivate joy and happiness every single day.
With my signature I confirm that I will take this practice seriously. With this signature I agree I will make myself a priority in my life."

_____
(sign your name on the line)

Let's dive in.

As mentioned earlier, cat lovers feel calmer when petting their cats and hearing the sound of their cat's purring. Their frequency has been scientifically proven to reduce blood pressure. It also relieves pain, heals wounds faster, and has other health benefits. This is not magic. It is science. **Sound vibration resonates at different levels measured**

by hertz. The higher the hertz frequency of the sound, the more benefits it can produce in the body. I dream of the day when animals are well accepted in hospitals so we can all receive the healing they want to share with us when we most need it.

How does frequency work in the body? The body is not a mass of dense static tissue. The body is composed of atoms in a constant state of motion and vibration. When the body is sick it means our vibration needs to be recalibrated. This is where frequency plays such an instrumental role in enabling this recalibration to occur.

Think for a moment about how our bodies relax when we listen to our favorite tunes; the music we listen to is a fantastic orchestration of multiple frequencies accelerating the atoms that make up the body. The higher those frequencies are, the better we feel. The opposite is true, as well. The lower the frequencies, the sadder we may also feel and the more prone to sickness we become, hence the correlation between low morale and vulnerability to sickness.

This is why songs can uplift our mood. The shift is instantaneous. Our mood changes the moment we hear our favorite tune come on the radio, or in our playlist, for example. Understanding this scientific concept can bring clarity to our minds as to why raising our frequency is so important for the health of our beloved animal companions and ourselves.

Each emotion we experience will indeed raise or reduce our unconditional love frequency. If we are feeling sad, anxious, depressed, or angry, our energy is very low. We are projecting with our bodies a non-healing energy that is not only to the detriment of those around us but also to ourselves. We can all relate to how we feel after spending time with a friend who was sad or depressed. Our body may have felt that low frequency emanating from our friend, and our unconditional love frequency, as a result, was lowered too.

Similarly, the opposite is also true. We all can remember how we felt the joy of a loved one. It felt contagious and before we knew it, we were feeling joyous too. It is all in the unconditional love frequency like the Wi-Fi waves. We know our emotions change when we are with someone who is happy or angry. We feel it. It is not our imagination.

Now we can understand why raising our unconditional love frequency is the number one step to working with animals. What kind of a disservice are we going to do to them if we show up with a low frequency from lower emotions such as anger, grief, apprehension, fear, or sadness?

Now that we have an idea about this superpower, what exactly do we do to raise our frequency so we can work with animals and with our loved humans?

I would like to provide some basic tools to be incorporated into our daily routine to raise our frequency. Let's consider this a Self-Love Guide. The compound effect of a self-love daily practice will create monumental changes in our unconditional love frequency over time. It is a snowball effect.

The good news is just as we may have suspected, we do not need to change. We just need to discard patterns that are harmful to our innate state of inner peace. How many babies have we seen that are not inherently happy? We are all born with that skill. It is our birthright. How are we supposed to do that in this crazy world we live in as adults? There is plenty we can do. We have choices. We are empowered.

It is not about learning; it is about *un*learning. All we need is our intention.

Let's dive into the foundation of happiness: self-love.

PART 4: PRACTICING OPENING OUR HEARTS

SELF-LOVE: WHERE TO BEGIN?

STEP 1: PRACTICE SELF-AWARENESS/JOURNAL EVERY DAY

Meditation each day for ten minutes trains our brains to calm down.

As we allow our minds to be quiet, we are able to start listening to what our hearts have to say. The heart is where our emotions are felt. A heavy heart will carry lower frequency emotions based on fear, anger, or sadness. A happy heart will carry higher frequency emotions such as satisfaction, serenity, empowerment, and joy.

By listening to our hearts every day, we can start discerning the emotions we are feeling in the moment and then take action to raise the unconditional love frequency again.

We can ask ourselves the question: **How do I feel in this moment?** Then, if we pause, the heart will speak. We will be able to label our emotion. Once the emotion has been identified, the next question to ask our heart is, **what do I need to feel better in this moment?** Then, pause. The heart has the answers. All we need is to practice stillness in order to listen to it.

When we do not carve out time to connect with ourselves and learn what we need to do to feel happier, we make the grave mistake of going through the day resonating at a low frequency that harms our body and the body of those around us in very subtle but quite real levels.

Another way to connect with what we need is journaling every day. There is no wrong way of journaling. We just need to take a notebook, a journal, or a piece of paper, and each day dedicate a space to ask, how do I feel in this moment? Listening to what the heart says and writing it down is the goal of journaling. This technique is recommended by therapists for effective self-discovery because knowing what and how we feel is the first step to identifying what we can do to feel better.

STEP 2: MASTERING OUR EMOTIONS

Now that we know *how* we feel, let's start building emotional resilience so we can pause at any given moment and *choose* how we want to respond to a challenging, unexpected, or annoying situation.

Let's think about an example of a stranger cutting in while we are in line to run an errand. There are a number of ways one can react. The lowest frequency reaction would be anger. But that is not the only way. The highest frequency response requires taking a moment to assess the situation and think calmly about how to rectify it in a way we can feel at ease again.

The difference here is knowing there is always a choice. If we give ourselves two seconds to seek composure before acting, we have the ability to choose to de-escalate or escalate the situation. The choice lies in the pause before the response. This is the key to mastering emotions.

As humans, we will go through an array of different emotions on any given day. That is what being human is all about. It is how we are designed to operate and find the richness in life's experiences. We all have diverse feelings, emotions, and frequencies. We just need to fine-tune them so we do not go to polar opposites depending on life's events. It is not a flaw; it is part of the human experience. All our emotions have a yin and a yang or our golden shadow and our dark shadow. Others may call it our virtues and our flaws.

However, this does not mean that everything that does not go the way our mind had initially expected has to bring us down or justify a low frequency reaction we will regret later. All it means is that **with great emotions, come great responsibility. We are the ones in charge of our emotions, not the other way around.**

The mastery is excruciatingly simple and yet not easy.

Pause.

Breathe.

Choose.

The day we pause before reacting is when we have mastered our emotions. We are not suppressing them, we are talking about always having the ability to stay in control, so the emotion does not control us. That comes with the pause, the breath, the choice.

Simple. Not easy.

It requires practice, daily practice. It requires diligence. It requires a mind that knows how to relax. This mindset begins with Step 1: Practice Self-Awareness/Journal Every Day. That pause is the moment when we choose *how* we want this experience to unfold. The pause is the game changer.

This story may provide us some additional insight into why mastering our emotions is an act of love to all the living beings who share this world with us. Our emotions do in fact have a strong impact on others whether we notice it or not. The key is to know this ahead of time, so we don't need to be sorry for letting our emotions get the best of us.

Here is a story of an animal who wants to remind us why **emotional accountability is crucial for the well-being of those around us**.

SCOLDED KITTY STORY

There was a time when a lady reached out to me because her indoor/outdoor kitty refused to come back inside the house. I inquired what had happened that made him stop coming inside. She said with a very regretful tone of voice that she had scolded him for bringing a dead mouse in the house.

She realized after the day of the scolding, he would go and get his food outside the house but would no longer come inside. This had gone on for about two weeks. She was getting worried that he may be potential prey for local predators.

I explained to her that a dead mouse is a cat's way of offering a precious gift as a sign of love to the humans in their life. They don't go to the store to buy a present. They go out in nature and spend a very serious amount of time observing, waiting, and hunting. Once they finally have their prized possession in their claws, they do not eat it: Those are intended as presents and brought to the human as offerings of love.

She felt really bad about not showing her appreciation for the cat's gift.

There you have it. I am an animal healing practitioner mediating a situation of feline hurt feelings and attempting to educate humans on the ways cats show their love. It is not always cuddles and purring. Sometimes it is dead animals and such.

I connected with the kitty, and I explained in images how regretful his human was. Humans are not always aware of the intent behind acts of love such as this one. The cat was very hurt. I felt a very heavy heart. It was as if the scolding for his gift was not just a dismissal of the effort he had put into hunting down the mouse, but was also a dismissal of his worth as a cat. So, the hurt feelings ran deep in his sweet feline heart.

Then, I spoke with the human again and asked her to make amends for what had happened. I asked her to do love offerings to the kitty in return so he would see that she was making an effort to reconcile. For the next few days, she would spend ten minutes of her time in meditation and holding in her heart the love she had for him, remembering him as he would walk in the door, eat a special treat, purr, or receive cuddles and loving pets. I recommended doing this every day until he chose to walk back inside and spend time with her again.

To her surprise, it did not take long. Within a few days I got word from the lady that her cat had come in. Then I recommended giving him special treats as a sign of reconciliation and gratitude.

WHAT I LEARNED FROM THIS KITTY CONNECTION

Animals get their feelings hurt as a result of our lack of emotional accountability. They teach us how important it is to be in control of our emotions in order to not hurt those we love. Animals included. With their behavior, they teach us how to be better human beings. They are our teachers.

STEP 3: LEARN THE IMPORTANCE OF SELF-REGULATION

What is self-regulation? I can explain this with a very simple example. Let's say we just had a very stressful commute. Do we have techniques we use to recalibrate ourselves so we can arrive to work calm? Or do we continue to feel stressed even though the commute has ended and we have already arrived?

Self-regulation is the process of bringing ourselves back to a neutral state. No matter the emotions our heart is experiencing due to a situation past or present, we have the ability to bring ourselves back to a neutral state before interacting with another being.

This is a lifelong commitment. Self-regulation is a practice. It means, we try again each day and commit to doing better. It means we practice Step 1 and Step 2, so we have the foundation that allows us to come back to our peaceful inner selves again. Self-regulation means we understand the world does not need to be problem-free for us to be calm.

For this, I recommend using emotional regulation apps such as Ahead: Emotions Coach or Clarity: CBT Thought Diary to play games, have fun, learn, and practice each day. Yes, we can read books on emotional intelligence and listen to podcasts or audio books to learn self-regulation. Yes, we can take online courses, and yes, we can seek therapy with a gamut of quite competent professionals. All of these are wonderful choices too. However, the power of daily micro-changes is built by consistent effort. **Our level of expertise is based on our consistency of the practice, not on the amount of reading we do**. It is not what we know that matters. It is what we do what makes all the difference.

Self-regulation is not a final destination. It is a journey. It means we will have days that are better than others. The important thing here is to commit to not repeating the same mistakes, to not allowing setbacks to derail us, to showing up each day and giving the best we can give that day without comparing ourselves to others. We are so worth it! Our happiness is worth it! We can do this; it's baby steps. There is no finish line; the reward is in showing up every single day. It is that easy!

STEP 4: LEARN COPING MECHANISMS

Coping mechanisms are tools that enable us to self-regulate. It can be something as simple as counting to ten before responding to the situation at hand that we know is challenging for us because it opens emotional wounds we have carried since childhood. It could be as simple as choosing to walk away from something too hard to handle in a peaceful manner.

It could be as simple as having a glass of water to ground ourselves. Feeling the hydrating sensation in our bodies can allow us to get out of our thoughts for a moment.

There are times when we need a pick-me-up, and we can use music to help us. We discussed in the previous chapter about how music can instantly change our frequency. Turning on music that always makes us happy and having a happy playlist at the ready can get us to shift that emotion in the moment. There will also be times when we need to self-regulate by acknowledging the sadness we carry and working on getting it out of our system. We can have a sad playlist also for when we need to release the tears we are bottling up. I personally binge watch very sad movies to cry as much as I can in one night and let all the sadness out. It is quite therapeutic. Psychiatrist Dr. Judith Joseph, author of the book called *High Functioning: Overcome Your Hidden Depression and Reclaim Your Joy*, recommends it. She covers in detail five building blocks to a happier life.

All of these are coping mechanisms. It would be a very wise strategy for us all to have a list of these in a note in our phones, posted on the fridge, on the first page of our journal, or any other place we can see daily. The best coping mechanisms are not the ones we have read about. The best ones are the ones we use daily. In order to use them daily, they need to be easily and readily accessible in the precise moment we need them.

Accessibility to our tools helps us to use them consistently. I have mine on my phone so I can always access them when I need them.

STEP 5: BRINGING PEACE TO THE MIND

This may come as a mind-blowing revelation to many of us—a very simple thing that we may have never thought about.

Let's imagine for a moment we are kids, and we got our hands on a delicious chocolate cake. We ate the whole thing! It was amazing! Afterwards, our stomachs were upset and we got sick. We learned very quickly not to eat an entire chocolate cake ever again.

As adults, think about all the indulgences we get ourselves into fully knowing the consequences to our mental health, emotional health, and overall well-being. Later, these consequences fuel our minds with thoughts of regret. Inevitably, our frequency plummets to the lowest levels—all fully preventable. We could have made different choices to prioritize well-being. We do them because of habit. It is time to acknowledge that bad habits make us prisoners of lower frequencies. We pay the consequences just like a kid suffering after indulging in an entire chocolate cake.

Instead, how about developing habits to promote positive states of serenity?

Habits that naturally clear the mind and bring us joy and peace are the better options to develop. We need habits that when put together make our experience on this Earth enjoyable. We need habits that build our lifestyle, which shapes our long-term happiness. When we are happy, we exude this happy energy to those around us; and who is around us all the time? Our beloved animal companions, or our beloved friends and family. They deserve to feel happy right? Then, what are we waiting for? Let's fill our cups so we can help fill theirs. They so deserve it! And so do we!

This story may very well illustrate how important it is to be able to bring peace to our hearts. When we reach a state of serenity by self-regulation and integrating coping mechanisms, we can help others around us to do the same. Our presence alone is all it takes.

EAGLE AT THE OREGON ZOO

Every year I go to the Oregon Zoo to do a Reiki energy offering to the animals who are living there instead of running wild in their natural habitats. I know no natural habitat is safe for any animal anymore, but I do feel zoos are the equivalent of human prisons. I practice my energy offering with the intent of lightening up the hearts of those animals who I know would be much happier roaming free in the forests, mountains, plains, rivers, and oceans.

On this particular day I was making my rounds to all the different zoo habitats and got to where the eagles were. All the eagles were looking at me during the healing session except one, perched on the other end of the enclosure and looking away from me. I noticed this eagle and I wondered: *Is it possible this eagle is unable to receive the unconditional love frequency I am sending?*

My curious mind inquired. As time went on and I was there for several minutes, I wanted to make sure all the eagles in the enclosure were able to benefit from the healing and use it for whatever purpose they chose. I then directed my attention to the one eagle looking away. In my mind, I asked her to please look at me if indeed she was receiving the energy healing. On the spot she did turn around and looked directly at me.

I remained quite humbled at that moment. She had very clearly and timely responded to my inquiry, and I felt happy she had acknowledged my offering.

MY LEARNING FROM THIS STORY

When in doubt, all we need to do is ask. Just like I mentioned earlier in a kitty story. Ask the animal what we need to know. Ask for a sign. Ask for a straight answer. The animal will respond in whichever way is easier for us to receive the message. In my case, I very specifically asked for that action to occur, and I knew without a doubt, I had received my answer.

We need to keep in mind that **animals are highly evolved creatures.** As such, they can choose if they want to receive our energy healing and when to receive it and for what purpose. They make all these choices, not us. In my early stages of animal healing, I first thought I knew what was best for them and I would be the one choosing where to send the energy and for what purpose. As I connected with animals at a deeper level and after I learned Shelter Animal Reiki, I realized animals know best how to utilize the energy they receive from our healing intentions.

Working with energy, I am open to infinite possibilities, and I work diligently on not reducing my practice to one expected outcome. I go in with only one goal: to be of service to the animal.

I would like to share what I have personally done to bring peace into my life. Yes, I certainly do all of this, not all at once but I do practice each of these things regularly. They have enriched my life to the point that my mind has little time to dedicate to lower frequency emotions such as fear or worry. That is the goal of this practice. The longer we hold a higher frequency, the more energy healing we share with our beloved animals and all the loved ones close to us.

I take this practice of detoxing from lower frequencies very seriously. I am fully aware how we are all bombarded every minute of the day with so much that brings us down. We owe it to ourselves and to our beloved animal companions to turn things around and to uplift ourselves with these strategies. We may choose one, two, or all of them. The key is to do it daily just like we might take a shower every day, eat our meals every day, and brush our teeth every day. Consistency is the key here. I hope we all can find at least one we will practice daily without fail. We will be so happy we did!

The following is an extensive list of my daily practice. Each of these examples is a practice in itself that brings tremendous benefits. I open the invitation to select one or two or more and perhaps over time, practice them all. The freedom lies in having choices because each day is different. One practice can be beneficial one day and another practice beneficial another day. Let's take note of the ones that resonate.

PART 4: PRACTICING OPENING OUR HEARTS

A. My highest priority is removing myself from toxic situations. There is enough going on in the world that I have no control over; therefore, I remove myself from the negative things I have control over, so they do not bring me down. Those times of enduring and doing what is expected of me are over. I do what I know is best for my well-being. I do so unapologetically and with zero regrets. I deserve to live in peace, and I make sure of it. This is by far the clearest boundary that I set with those around me.

B. Declutter my physical space regularly. There is a connection between the brain's healthy functioning and the clean and organized physical space around us. The more uncluttered space we have, the clearer our thoughts are. There is a subconscious communication taking place in the brain. The clutter signals to the brain, "I need to clean this" every single time we pass by that area. It is not a conscious thought. It is a signal triggered so many times in a day that by the end of the day we may feel drained, and we do not even know why. This is why having a clear space is reenergizing for us. An uncluttered space sends a subconscious signal to the brain that we like the space. Our brains are incredible machines operating at the conscious, subconscious, and unconscious levels. They never rest.

C. Eliminate news that provokes anxiety and depression. Also, any other programming that promotes fear, grief, anger, or other low frequency emotions should be avoided. In my life, having knowledge of horrific things happening in the world has never empowered me to make the world a better place. Quite the opposite. It gives me a feeling of hopelessness, which is a very low frequency emotion I do not need to intentionally bring into my life. I watch news to inform and inspire me, and then I can take action toward solutions. This is a phenomenal catalyst to raising our unconditional love frequency. We need to consider other sources of information we may need to feel plugged into the happenings of the world. For example, www.positive.news is a good alternative. At all costs, we should avoid doomscrolling.

D. Be in nature every day. I walk every day I spend time surrounded by trees, a creek, and wildlife, and I admire the sky, clouds, sunrise, and sunset. This recharges me, invigorates me, and resets my thoughts to a state of pure serenity. Do we have parks near where we live? Do we have open spaces? How often do we visit these? Perhaps we take the bike or the car and head out to the nearest one or explore a faraway one each weekend. The variation in geology, scenic landscapes, and biodiversity in all levels of nature is so rich and wonderful. Any moment we spend away from nature can lead the body to feel less alive. I feel strongly about being in nature. Kayaking, climbing, hiking, bird watching, kite flying, mountain biking, or just sitting by a tree surrounded by nobody but nature are all ways to ground and feel more peaceful.

E. I practice self-care daily: I bring nutritious foods to my body so it can be recalibrated to homeostasis, its natural state of well-being and well-functioning. I prioritize exercise and sleep to provide my body and my mind the most foundational pillars for great health. I take time to listen to music that is harmonious and relaxes my nervous system. I also prioritize doing more of the things that make me happy rather than the things others expect of me.

PART 4: PRACTICING OPENING OUR HEARTS

F. I am selective of the circle of people around me. This includes both family and friends. The question comes down to this: Do I feel uplifted when I spend time with them, or do I feel down? If they uplift me, they will remain in my close circle. If they don't, I will practice distancing. I want to always feel uplifted just as they expect to feel uplifted after seeing me. Practicing discernment with all the people around me is one of the most crucial components of my self-care. There will be times when something happened causing them to be in a lower frequency. That is life. I am referring to the majority of the times I see them. Where is their energy? I pay attention to this to set a healthy boundary for the sake of my well-being.

G. Community, according to a Harvard study on happiness, is the number one reason we are happy. The connection we create by being in a community of like-minded people fulfills our most primal need in human life. I have multiple communities who share the same interests I have. They can be as diverse as volunteering for the cause of animals I love so much, or related to sports that make me feel so alive with every drop of sweat we share together, or a group that learns or discovers together. Community brings people together for a common purpose. Spending time together with a shared interest fulfills us as humans. The more often we practice this, the higher our frequency will remain.

Let's please take a moment and brainstorm about what communities we already have and perhaps choose a new one to be part of that will bring us joy. Perhaps leave one and start another one that is more aligned with our values and interests. This is important. Let's not wait another second.

H. Allowing our creative process to work freely is a magnificent way to also raise our unconditional love frequency. Perhaps we enjoy writing, taking photographs, building things, sculpting, coloring, painting, singing, writing music, creating art, geometry, planting, or gardening. All these are examples of our marvelous creative power. It is a wondrous thing to birth something new into the world that did not exist before. The more we create, the more we live in a higher unconditional love frequency.

I. Travel: I travel regularly. Visiting new places, meeting new people, and experiencing different cultures gives an incredible boost to my psyche and to my heart. I feel more alive when I learn new things, when I explore new places. It is the most sublime experience of aliveness I can feel as a human being. I recommend travel to expand perspectives, understand cultures better, appreciate other types of beautiful scenery, and feel fully alive. Travel to me is one of the highest frequencies I can experience. It does not have to be internationally. The key is experiencing a new place. It brings us back to that state of wonder of a childlike perception.

J. Sound Baths: I regularly do crystal bowls or gong sound baths. The vibration I feel in my body as these beautiful instruments are played can only be described as having a massage from the inside of my body. It is as if I can tell every cell in every organ and every tissue and bone mass of my body feels happy. Beneficial Sound by Wayne Marto also offers weekend retreats, and this is the ultimate spa experience for my soul, mind, and body. I feel absolutely

PART 4: PRACTICING OPENING OUR HEARTS

rejuvenated after these sessions. I highly recommend incorporating a monthly or a regular session like these to recalibrate vibration frequently.

K. Use gadgets to shield from sensory overload. Recently, I have grown quite sensitive to external stimuli. Lights seem much brighter to my sensitive eyes; loud noises feel like an assault to my nervous system. I now have earplugs and sunglasses I wear daily to mitigate this stimuli intensity that disrupts my physical comfort. If there are stimuli that also disrupt our peace, let's find ways to mitigate or eliminate them so this constant discomfort does not lower our frequency.

L. Practice gratitude daily. Many, many years ago, my daughter gave me a book for Christmas. There were 365 entries of gratitude spaces intended to be done daily so by the end of the year I would have 365 reasons to be grateful. I started doing the first few pages for the first week and I quickly realized I was being repetitive. I was grateful for my daughter, my friends, my job, and my home. I challenged myself to think differently and be thankful for different things each day without repeating.

What this practice showed me is that all of life is an infinite tapestry of beautiful experiences to be thankful for. I started writing things like the following:

Today I am grateful I made time to have a super fun Zumba or Hip Hop workout that made me happy and made my body healthier.

Today I am grateful for the person in the store who chose to make eye contact and engage with me with a smile making my shopping experience a much more pleasant one.

Today I am grateful my brain generated such great ideas that are already making my job easier.

Today I am thankful I followed my intuition and avoided getting into a challenging situation.

Today I am grateful I got out of bed even though I felt like it was going to be a long day, but I chose to show up.

Fast forward to today, this practice is now so intrinsically embedded in my daily life that not a moment goes by when I am not deeply grateful for the experience of being alive to enjoy the moment unfolding in front of me. These are very simple things like drinking a cup of tea that warms my body and brings a pleasant aroma to my room or enjoying a meal of vegetables and grains that were planted, grown, and harvested under the sunshine, capturing the nutrients of the soil that will then nourish my body. Another is being grateful for the air I am breathing that goes into my healthy lungs which are not polluted to the point where I am going to be sick. I go through so many things that are not material objects but experiences of my day. Also, I am grateful because I know I am constantly guided, protected, and loved by Source, by all of creation.

Gratitude is truly a game changer. If out of all these lifelong habits we need to choose one to start with, let's choose gratitude. It will open the door to a fresh new perspective of life, and this is the fertilizer that will nourish our creative power beyond what we can imagine. Let's try it right now. What are five things to be thankful for right here, right now? Next, let's challenge ourselves to write five more. It is a fun practice. Gratitude is truly infinite—as infinite as there are possibilities, and as infinite as there are stars.

> M. I connect with my higher power each day. I listen to my heart. I meditate and go within. I take a long moment to

truly be in a state of pure tranquility where I can have direct communication with Spirit, with Source, with the Earth, with my angels and spirit guides, my ancestors, and the different higher frequency beings who work with me. I connect to their wisdom and receive their unconditional loving energy. This connection balances me, grounds me, and propels me into the beginning of the day. Every single day. The inner gentle voice can only be heard in stillness.

N. Recently I started practicing circular breath work. This technique has had a very impactful effect on me. Circular breath work is continuously breathing without pausing between inhalation and exhalation. It is a constant flow under the loving guidance of the breath work facilitator. These sessions changed the chemistry of my body. My vagus nerve is now regulated. My stress hormones have been reduced, my brain fog completely disappeared, and my body buzzes with energy as if I were fifteen again. There is a spiritual quality to this energy flow in the body that makes me more connected to the oneness of it all. The universal force in our heart is felt in my entire body. It is a very spiritual experience and all I need to do is breathe. Breath of Gold is the website where I signed up for this wonderful, guided breath work practice.

O. Dancing for me has always been a fantastic way of channeling joy through movement. I smile, I dance to the beat of favorite tunes, and I feel more alive than ever. Dancing in community is an even greater gift. There is something about the moment when we look at our dance partner and it feels like their soul is dancing to the beat of the music. It is absolutely priceless. Dancing for the joy of dancing is another spiritual experience. I fully recommend it to everyone! It doesn't matter if we are coordinated or not. The point is not to do it right; the point is to feel the frequencies pulsate in our body and uplift us. Hip Hop Hiits (Hip Hop High Intensity Interval Training) are my dancing sisters, and I love dancing with them. It feeds my soul with unconditional love.

P. Getting up early and taking just a few minutes of my day to sync up with the cycle of the Earth kicks off my day with serenity. I admire the colors around me, look up, and see the immense vastness of the sky. I appreciate the changes from one day to the other, from one minute to the next. It is ethereal; it is a spiritual experience. It is a moment when nature stays still; and we are all in sync witnessing the miracle of life starting all over again. I pay attention to the mystical silence that takes place during the golden hour. What a beauty this is, and those who stay in bed do not even comprehend how miraculous this is. Those of us who make a point to get out of bed for it feel rewarded with something far more than just a beautiful sunrise; we are rewarded with the gift of connection with life itself. It is absolutely magical. If we are not morning people and this sounds nearly impossible to do, let's try perhaps one day a week and see how we feel. The benefits may propel us to make it a more regular practice later on.

Q. Reading is another one of my practices. I read books on all topics to nourish my soul not just my brain. I have the entire day to fill my brain with data, do problem solving, organization, coordination, planning, and more. I use my free time to acquire wisdom instead: shift perspectives, grow, feel inspired, and become a happier version of myself. I choose books to foster wisdom. My choices are uplifting and inspirational. There is of course the occasional exception that I call brain candy. This satisfies a desire towards a specific topic or literary genre. However, these are few and far between. My free time is limited, and I feel more drawn toward self-expansion in this moment of my life.

R. I practice changing my perspective. Here is an illustration provided by a psychology professor to his students. He held an empty glass in front of his students and asked them the question: "Is the glass empty?" All the students responded, yes. But he told them, "It is not true; it is full of air." Then he proceeded to place as many marbles as he could fit in the glass. Again, he asked his students, "Is the glass full now?" They all responded yes. But alas, everyone was wrong. The professor grabbed sand with his hand and placed as much sand in the glass as he could fit in there. And then asked again: "Is the glass full?" All the students said yes. The students could not imagine anything else fitting in that glass, but the professor was able to fill it up even more. This time he added water. And the story goes to show that there are many perspectives, not just one. If we only allow ourselves to have an open mind, we will be able to see clearly the infinite possibilities available every step of the way. Shifting perspectives is one of the practices I work on every single day. It is liberating. I recommend you try it too!

In summary, we have the ability to raise our frequency to unconditional love by making these choices in our day-to-day life. The list I share is just my list. I invite all of us to create our very own list in order to establish a discipline of raising our frequency every day. These choices may seem small like selecting music we love instead of listening to upsetting news. Choices may be bigger like finally distancing ourselves from that person who is consistently bringing us down. In the end, it is the daily practice of pause, breathe, and choose that allows us to reach a state of self-awareness. This presence in the now moment will in turn allow us to become proficient in controlling our emotions, so the emotions no longer control us. It is then that mastery of our energy happens. The variety of strategies available gives us a vast number of possibilities. All we need to do is try them out and find what suits us best. What works for one person may not necessarily work for another. The key is in trying, exploring, and then choosing what resonates with us. Then sticking with it day after day to integrate it in our lifestyle. The benefits of the practice of unconditional love are infinite. It works in so many marvelous ways. This practice will open the door to extraordinarily transformational experiences.

In thirty days, let's take note of the changes we have noticed. At that thirty-day mark, we can decide to incorporate one more strategy and work on it for the following thirty days, then take note again of what changes have occurred. As we start realizing the positive outcome of our effort, we will be motivated to keep integrating more and more strategies until one day we realize, our life has shifted 180 degrees, and we have become a much happier version of ourselves.

To get there, it is crucial to start with the commitment of trying just one strategy and truly sticking with it. We have lots to gain and nothing to lose! I hope we choose happiness over the comfort of not making the effort. In the end, the choice is all ours. We are in control of our journey. Would we give happiness a chance? After all, if we intend to work with animals, with the beautiful Mother Earth, or with other humans, raising our own frequency through personal practice is the very first step toward personal mastery.

PART 5
EXUDING HEALING ENERGY: OUR ANIMAL COMPANIONS WILL BE GRATEFUL!

If we have the honor of enjoying the unconditional love of an animal companion in our home or perhaps our farm, we may feel inspired to work on cultivating a heart-centered life filled with unconditional love in order to share that loving frequency with our beloved animals. Working with energy everyday through mastery is nothing short of miraculous. Through the years of being with animals during their passing, illness, and other challenging moments, I have witnessed how rebalancing energy brings about the most unexpected results. The following stories may open our eyes and hearts to what we could witness should we choose to practice the techniques I share in this chapter.

HOPE, THE CHILDLESS HORSE

We may need a tissue box before continuing; this story always makes me cry.

Years ago, I was part of an awesome spiritual group that focused on bringing energy healing to the Earth in places that had experienced severe trauma like war zones, genocide, massacres, unspeakable crimes, animal cruelty, and more. We did this regularly as a group to put our gifts together to make this world a happier place and release the trauma that stays imprinted in the geographical location where it occurred. Imagine going to Gettysburg and not feeling the heaviness of this place in every cell in your body. Many of us have visited places that make us cringe. It was these places we chose to direct our loving energy for the highest good of the land and the souls inhabiting it.

The leader of this group, who has now passed, connected me to a Canadian rescue horse sanctuary. This place had over eighty horses, all of which had been saved from slaughter.

My friend asked me if I could work on a white horse she had just rescued that was in very critical condition. She had taken her to the vet, and she did not think she was going to survive. I connected to the horse remotely. I learned that she had had several babies and every single time, the babies had been taken away from her. She was an older mare, and she felt heartbroken that the joy of motherhood had been robbed from her youth. She so longed to be a mother and share life with a little one. Animals have very deep feelings. Just like humans, they connect deeply with others. She had no desire to keep living because of this void in her heart.

In my energy healing session, I encouraged her to keep living, to see a brighter future ahead of her now that she had been rescued. I wanted her to know she was safe, and she would be in a much happier emotional place living with other horses. She would be able to finally thrive, I told her. I kept in touch with the lady to get updates on her. Her health started to get better. It felt as if she was going to make it after all. But that was not the most amazing thing that happened. Not only did she survive the animal cruelty she had endured, but she also healed from all the physical conditions she had. She was thriving, galloping in the field with the other horses. She was starting to enjoy life for the first time. This wonderful lady named her Hope.

Energy healing always works in the highest and greatest good and in ways our human mind most of the time cannot anticipate. Here is the part that warms my heart the most.

Months later, another mare had a baby. After the birth of the baby, Hope became a second mother to her. The two mares walk alongside the baby wherever she decides to go. Hope never leaves her side. The biological mother loves the baby, but Hope loves her even more. She represents for her all the babies that were taken away from her. She represents the hope and desire to live that she had lost.

When I got to see them together, I was so moved by that sight. Hope, with whom I connected remotely, had given up on life, and now she is thriving and experiencing the joys of motherhood. Wow! I never knew energy healing could contribute to this beautiful miracle. I don't ever know how the energy will work to create, release, facilitate, change, or transform. It is always a very humbling experience for me to witness the beauty of divine essence at work. This is what unconditional love does, and it has the power to change the world when we all learn to live in this frequency every day.

What melts my heart is that I don't have to speak horse language. All I need to do is to have an open heart that transmits unconditional love. Hope understands me perfectly well, and I understand her too. Isn't that amazing? The only language that truly communicates without fear of misinterpretation is the language of higher frequency love.

Just imagine if we can communicate with animals with love, why can't we do the same with humans, and avoid friction, hurt feelings, and unnecessary drama? I believe we owe it to ourselves to use unconditional love more in our day-to-day communication with others, whether they are animals or humans; we can see for ourselves the results we get.

I want to mention one more detail that also makes me tear up. When I arrived at the sanctuary, Hope was nowhere in sight, she was in the pasture far away. She somehow sensed I was there in the sanctuary, and she knew who I was. She came galloping toward me and stopped in front of me. I knew at that moment she was elated to see me. How incredibly cool for her to come running to see me without being called! I took it as a sign of her deep gratitude for being there for her to give her a nudge so she would not give up on life. Connection with animals fills my heart with such incredible joy. This moment is so vivid in my memory, I sense Hope's love in my heart every so often. I love her!

WHAT I LEARNED FROM HOPE

Nothing is impossible when we have unconditional love in our hearts. Hopeless things can turn around and show us that miracles are possible, and they happen every single day! Hope is a prime example of that!

MOLLY, HORSE KIDNAPPED IN CANADA

This is quite possibly the most extraordinary experience I have had as an animal energy healing practitioner up to this moment.

It happened in October 2018. I was on a spiritual trip in France when I received a call from my friend, who led the spiritual group I mentioned before. She said that we had an animal to help—Molly, a Clydesdale. She was kidnapped from her sanctuary overnight and the staff and volunteers were frantically looking for her. It all pointed to someone coming into the sanctuary, and out of all the horses there, specifically taking Molly because of her muscular body. There is an illegal market of horse meat in Canada. The horse meat is exported to Japan.

From where I was in France, I connected with this horse I have never met before to try to get clues as to her whereabouts. Typically, I do not work on locating missing animals. Regardless, it was absolutely worth giving it a try if it meant we could get her back to her safe place. I saw the kidnapping moment as if it was a movie playing in my mind. There, she was led by two men, one older and one younger; it felt like they were father and son. They put her in a horse trailer pulled by a very large Ram pickup truck. I only saw the men from behind. It was the view Molly had when being taken.

I saw a house in the countryside. There was a porch all around the house. It was a pretty house not surrounded by any other houses. I could not see any street signs or numbers that could be identifiers of the location. It was clearly the countryside. I saw how Molly went into a very small one-stall barn where she had no light. She was in the dark in a very small area. I felt her uneasiness turning into fear. She felt scared being in the dark and away from the horses she knew in the sanctuary.

Connecting with her I could feel what she felt when she was taken. But how was that going to help get the sanctuary people enough information to find her location? I felt so sad about this. I wanted to help, but I could not see the situation from a human perspective to get her address. I was seeing the situation from Molly's eyes only, her experience and her emotions.

Three other friends and I from the same spiritual group kept connecting. We would get a view of the field nearby and the look of the country road leading to the field. We also sensed her proximity but not her exact coordinates.

A rescue team was organized to start searching in all countryside areas near the sanctuary that fit the description of the house, the pickup truck, and the small barn. There were a number of places that fit the description, and the search team was looking. My spiritual group friends were also receiving information from Molly and her proximity, but again, no solid coordinate identifiers. It is hard. It is a vast open space. How do we describe what we see to the point where we lead others to her location?

I connected with Molly again to see if she was doing OK given the circumstances. She was starting to fade away as if she was hopeless and did not want to keep going. Animals can lose the desire to live, and she was reaching that point. I then told her we were searching and to please make noise with her strong hind legs when she sensed the search team nearby so we could find her. I asked her to please kick that barn door open to free herself and run so the search team could see her. I also saw she had an ethereal white horse above her giving her courage and strength so she would not give up. It must have been her own horse spirit guide. I felt peace in my heart knowing she was guided, and she was not alone.

The search continued. But those who kidnapped her were very afraid she would be found on their property, so they transported her to another location and then another. For the search team, and for those of us trying to help remotely, this complicated things. We would get close to Molly and then, we would have to start all over again.

Due to all the attention this kidnapping was getting in the community, the kidnappers were seriously worried they would not be able to auction her and get the money they wanted to pay whatever debts they had. They were not thieves. This was not something they typically did. They did this criminal act out of financial despair and lack of love for animal life. They quickly realized what a serious mistake they had made.

Almost three months later, on Christmas Eve, the sanctuary owners left the sanctuary to spend Christmas with their daughter in the city.

To their astonishment, something they never imagined had happened. Molly was back in her stall upon their return.

Imagine their surprise when they saw their kidnapped horse safe and back in her place. There was no note to explain how she made it back. Clearly, she had been brought back by those who stole her. It was Christmas Eve, three months after she had been kidnapped.

Molly showed signs of being pregnant. She must have been pregnant before she left, and it had been too early to be noticeable. Horse pregnancies last eleven months. Not only had she been returned safely, but she was also going to have a baby. Double surprise!

Soon we all heard the news of this incredible story. Molly was back! We all felt such a sense of relief and joy. What a miracle! Never in a million years did I ever imagine this could even happen. But it did!

This is what I love about energy healing with animals. The energy I send doesn't have a specific outcome or intention in mind. I send it freely to be utilized by the animal in the way the animal chooses for their highest and greatest good and of all involved. My human mind cannot comprehend all the infinite possibilities. But I trust the animal will know how to best direct the energy being received.

This story always makes me tear up for all the obvious reasons of heartwarming Christmas miracles taking place. Also, because Molly taught me to never have expectations when holding the frequency of unconditional love. I was focusing so much on Molly's well-being, but little did I know that this energy would soften the hearts of these two men to the point they chose to return her unharmed. Emotionally traumatized yes, but physically unharmed. These men had meant to cause her harm when they first took her from her home. That change of heart was made possible with unconditional love energy being poured on Molly. The side effect of that is what freed her in the end. Taking the risk of being caught in the act, the kidnappers had returned to the scene of their crime to make right their wrongdoing.

Of course, I had to visit this sanctuary and meet Molly in person! I chose to go in spring after Molly's baby was born. I was blessed enough to encounter beautiful sunny weather while I was there and enjoy this marvelous visit that filled my heart with joy forever.

I met Molly, her baby, and guess who else I got to meet in this sanctuary?

Hope, the white horse!

It is Molly's baby that Hope bonded with and both Molly and Hope raised that baby together: Moxie.

This is truly the most remarkable animal story! It was the work of my friends and me together. Extraordinary things happen when we hold the frequency of love. I say with the most absolute certainty, miracles happen every day because I see them happen every single day. Life itself is a miracle! We have just grown accustomed to taking miracles for granted. But they are happening every day! This one was no exception. The only difference is that it was such a happy outcome for all involved, it will be in my books as the most special animal miracle of all. Up to this point anyway! I know there are more miracles in the making right here, right now, and I plan on being part of many of them too!

My hope, dearest reader, is that this story opens our hearts to not only believe, but to know that yes, miracles are not only possible, but they do happen every day.

WHAT MOLLY TAUGHT ME

Hold unconditional love energy toward something or someone and allow things to unfold in whichever way is the highest and greatest good for all. **Be open to the infinite possibilities**. Forget about expectations. Forget about specific outcomes. Allow love to surprise us like it surprised my friends and me.

I hope these stories have given us all inspiration to be a beacon of light for the animals. Farm animals, wild animals, domestic animals, and captive animals: all are beautiful, sentient beings eager to receive loving energy.

HOW CAN WE ALL BRING MORE UNCONDITIONAL LOVE FREQUENCY INTO THE WORLD OF ANIMALS?

Perhaps by now some of us may be wondering what we can do to make this world a better place for animals. What follows is truly my wish list of things we can all do to honor the beautiful presence of animals in this world. I provide them as suggestions. These are things I do personally. We can pick one or two or all of these. The choice is ours. The animals will be so grateful!

FOOD SUPPLY

Let's start with the food supply, shall we? How much meat does the human body need to be healthy? In many cases zero. But each body is different and has different needs. So, it would not be realistic to imagine we would or should all go vegan overnight. However, the so-called quality of the animal protein we consume is nutritionally compromised by the conditions in which the animal lives until they go to the slaughterhouse. For this reason, learning about plant-based protein options to have healthier nutrition in our diet would be wonderful. The less demand for meat, the fewer factory farms there will be.

The consumer demand is what drives the factory farm economic model. However, if we cannot see ourselves becoming vegetarian or vegan, that is perfectly understandable. The next best thing is to personally visit the place where our meat comes from and see for ourselves the conditions in which these animals live. That means, eat only local so we can verify those labels we read. Sales and marketing can be very sly with their wording, and people may not be buying what they think they are buying. We should visit the farm and see for ourselves if the animals are truly well taken care of. Happy animals mean healthy protein. Sick and sad animals mean unhealthy protein. By adjusting our lifestyle, all of us may improve our health and the life of hundreds of thousands of animals. The next best thing is to purchase from the small farmers who come to the farmers' market nearby. They raise those animals themselves. We can talk to them, learn from them, and then make the choice that feels right.

INJURED ANIMALS

When we see a hurt animal on the road, I would hope that we would not only help but also remember how powerful love is and bathe the animal in unconditional love rather than sorrow and pity. Yes, it sounds impossible, but it is quite possible. If I can do it, so can all of us. Shifting perspective is the key to doing this in moments of agonizing pain.

The way I explain shifting perspectives to my students is as follows. Our minds have the tendency to focus on the sadness of the moment, which is one way of looking at the situation at hand. But there are other ways. What if we exclusively focus on how much we love this animal and imagine it being happy, healthy, and unharmed? After all, we are bringing comfort to the animal. We do not want to bathe them in pity.

Do we know of anyone who feels comforted when being told how terrible the situation they are in is? We all feel comforted when someone finds a way of making us see a brighter side of things. So, this is basically the same with animals. We will not use words; we will use love and not pity. Perhaps they will live, perhaps they won't, but the love we provide in that moment makes all the difference in comforting them and easing them into the possible crossing of the rainbow bridge.

When we encounter animals that have already passed, let's do the same as above. Picture the animal in our minds being happy, united with others of their kind, and in a state of bliss. This small gesture of love can help the animal move on. Sometimes their souls linger nearby because they are caught between staying with what (and who) they know and moving on to the other realm. This act of holding the vision of their happiness allows them to transition. Shifting perspectives takes diligent daily practice. The benefits of the practice are what help us perform this act of love in heartbreaking moments like this.

Here is a story that shook me when it happened. As I reflect on the wisdom I received, I realize how energy works in incredibly mysterious ways. Never could I have imagined my role as an energy healing practitioner who could help animals cross the rainbow bridge in this way.

DEER CROSSING THE HIGHWAY

I was driving to Southern Oregon, and I had a very real apprehension in my heart because I was going to be driving during twilight when wildlife is most active and chances of them crossing the road increase exponentially. This is a fact. But this particular day I could not leave work any earlier, and indeed, I got caught driving as the day transitioned into night.

Halfway into the journey, I was driving in the right lane followed by a semi. To my left, a car was passing. In the middle of the highway was a concrete divider, the type that makes a very solid barrier between the two directions of highway traffic. To my dismay, there he was. A deer. Seconds felt like eternity. I saw the deer caught in a dilemma: run towards the left or run towards the right. I saw the deer's eyes, and I knew he had decided to go in my direction. I looked at the semi driving behind me, and I realized I could not hit my brakes or the semi would run me over. I could not swerve to the left because of the car passing me. So, I swerved to the right slightly so I would not fall off the highway and down the hill. As I feared, the deer could not cross fast enough, and I did hit him.

My heart sank. I cried as I kept driving. I did not see him at all in my rearview mirror. I was 100 percent certain he had fallen off the hill. I felt a deep sense of sadness. I am an animal lover and an animal energy healer, and I could not prevent this death. I was shaking. I was so shocked by what had just happened in the split of a second. Just that fast, I had quickly assessed what options I had, what options the deer had, and the deer had chosen me to be the one to hit him. As I write this story tears still flood my eyes.

I needed to know why he picked me. The deer had a choice. Why me?

I asked him with an open heart and received his message. The deer was ill and was going to have a slow death. He seized the opportunity to die quickly. It was a choice between dying slowly from a physical illness or dying quickly by getting a fatal hit. I was the one he chose to make it happen.

Once I inspected my car for the inevitable damage that this accident had caused, I found zero signs of the hit. No blood, no dents, no nothing. My car was intact. I know people who have had their cars totaled by hitting a deer. Here I was, not even a scratch. It was as if this hit had not even happened. The deer had chosen me to bring him a quick death and the deer had returned the favor by not causing any damage to the car. I do consider that to be quite extraordinary.

WHAT I LEARNED FROM THIS STORY

Miracles happen every day. Inexplicable things happen every single day. Sometimes sad endings occur. This too is part of the magical and extraordinary cycle of life.

As we embrace life, we also need to embrace death for **there is deep wisdom in the transition of one realm into the other.**

STOP HUNTING

If we hunt as a sport, let's please consider stopping. This is not truly a game when the animal is running for their life. It reminds me of the time when the Christians were hunted by the lions in the Roman Colosseum to entertain the Roman emperors. I am quite sure those humans being hunted never felt that to be a sport. I would have to say it had to be horrendously terrifying to run for their lives for people's entertainment. We humans have so many ways of finding entertainment. Wouldn't it be much nicer to find a hobby that does not involve causing harm to a living being? It may not seem wrong, but the heart knows it is. In the end, it will weigh heavy in the heart one day. Why not change now so as not to carry that burden later? I know I may be asking too much based on beliefs, society's norms, or upbringing. I do hope the animals' perspective can be considered and then let our hearts tell us the right path to follow.

HONOR ANIMALS DAILY

Let's honor the animals on a daily basis by sending them love from the comfort of our homes. Perhaps sit in meditation and send love to all the animals flying in the sky, may their path be safe from danger, may their air be healthy and free from toxins, may their food supply be clean and nourishing. We can continue with the animals and fish in the sea. May they find clean waters to provide nourishment and a safe place to enjoy their lives. Then the animals in the land, in the savannas, mountains, burrows, forests, deserts, underground, zoos, farms, factory farms, shelters, homes, laboratories, and in any other location. Let's imagine them all being happy, free from harm, healthy, and connected to their kind. We can imagine, just that, imagine. Then we can hold in our hearts a deep sense of love for them—for their diversity, their beauty, and their essence. Just holding that feeling in our hearts and projecting it as if we were a lighthouse casting a very wide beam of light onto all these beings in all these locations is enough to make a difference.

If we practice this regularly, we can imagine the changes our unconditional love frequency can create in the world.

And of course, we can do it in person too!

EDUCATE AND ADVOCATE

We can visit animals in all these locations too by getting involved and becoming a volunteer at a shelter or sanctuary, the zoo, or assisting on a farm. Farmers can always use an extra hand. We can become activists to be the voice of the animals. If all of this seems too much, sharing the love remotely is perfect too! Dedicating time each day or each week to sending loving energy to a group of animals is an excellent way to make their world a better place.

Spreading the word to friends and family and others about animal cruelty and abuse is a great way to help others make choices in the best interest of the animals and ourselves. We have many powers to use, like our financial power. If cruelty is not a profitable business, the industry will be forced to change or choose to go bankrupt. We can use the power of word of mouth; we can share our stories, so others know what we know and make an educated change for the better. With the power of love, we can give animals love to help them navigate this world with a little bit more ease and less suffering.

Animals are wonderful, they are worth our effort and time. Let's start now! The animals will be grateful!

I hope we find the following stories from my visits to the farm animal sanctuaries inspiring. They have profoundly changed me.

FARM ANIMAL SANCTUARIES

I visit sanctuaries often. I have been doing it for many years now.

I want to be in the presence of animals as much as I can. I want to bring them my energy healing as I clean their stalls, coops, and living areas. They are always so grateful and so incredibly loving.

Someone who has never been with a cow will never understand how much like a puppy they behave. They love their scratches; they follow me for a treat. They close their eyes and let me pet them for as long as I want. Someone who has not interacted with a pig will not understand how incredibly smart and playful they are. They follow me and roll on their backs to get their belly rubbed, just like a dog does. They are so clean! I go into their stalls, and they never soil the area of the stall where they sleep. Never.

Someone who has not been around geese or turkeys or chickens will not understand how much they love to be in our company and receive our touch. They love to be picked up by gentle loving hands and to be wrapped in someone's arms and rest their neck on their shoulders. The rooster might fly to be on my shoulder just because he wants to be with me. No other reason. No other purpose. They just desire our loving company.

The goats and the sheep will surround us as we clean their barn and be close to us to enjoy our presence. Their bodies will relax, and they may soon just fall sound asleep with no care in the world: in complete trust, in complete surrender—even though they all had in their psyche an indelible mark of how cruel humans can be. I find that in itself is the biggest miracle of all: watching all these rescued animals trust again, something humans struggle to do after we endure our own trauma in our lives.

WHAT I HAVE LEARNED BY WORKING WITH FARM ANIMALS IN SANCTUARIES

All animals are marvelous creations of the divine force that resides on Earth. No animal exists by mistake. No animal is here without a soul. None. Each of their lives is precious. Each of them brings something exceptionally unique to the larger tapestry of wondrous marvels of nature, just like each human does. They are an infinite source of joy and my heart truly expands when I get to be with them.

With this honor also comes great responsibility. These animals residing in sanctuaries have gone through very cruel, abusive, and neglectful situations, and many times I listen to the heartbreaking stories of the activists who heroically rescued them from their horrendous living conditions to have a better life at the sanctuary. Sometimes, a person's heart does open and they suddenly realize how cruel this world can be for them. Until everyone's hearts open, it is our responsibility to lead by example. In a world of pain, we can be hope. In a world of suffering, we can be love. That is a big responsibility. But we can do it!

CHARLOTTE, THE ANGUS COW

Here is a truly heartwarming animal story.

It was a typical rainy winter morning and there I was getting all muddy and dirty helping out with the cleaning duties at the sanctuary. I did not grow up on a farm. I learned all my duties by helping at the sanctuary as an adult. There is something to be said about being out

PART 5: EXUDING HEALING ENERGY

in the open space away from buildings, cars, and people, and breathing fresh air. It is called peace. When arriving at the sanctuary, I feel like the hecticness of the week washes away. As I enter and see all the animal faces, I feel at home. I smile. They of course smile in their hearts because they too are happy to see me. It is not that I bring treats since most of the time I do not come with a bag full of fruit. They are happy I am there. Fruit or not. The sincere and genuine appreciation for my showing up is the best thank you anyone can ever give me.

One morning turned out to be extra special. The sanctuary owner showed us a new member of the family who was all by herself in a stall with a few blankets on. She had yet to be vaccinated so we needed to be careful not to bring our harmful human germs to this delicate and fragile baby that may or may not make it. She was under special care because of the circumstances of her so-called birth.

She was only a few days old, and she was brought to this sanctuary by a man who was taking cows to the slaughterhouse and realized this one cow was pregnant. He is clearly not an animal rights activist by any stretch of the imagination, but something in his heart told him to rescue the near-death unborn baby. So he did. But not knowing how to take care of a calf and what to do, he took the calf to his home and placed her on his bed. He truly wanted to give this baby an opportunity to live.

After a few days, he found the sanctuary and took the calf there. We were in awe at how tiny and adorable she was, and we all felt the sadness of her forced birth. She was saved as her mom was killed and she never got to milk from her or have that bond babies have with their moms. Animals have feelings and emotions, and I could see she was sad. She had tears rolling down constantly, and I knew how alone she felt in this world without that sense of safety a mother provides to a defenseless newborn. She may not have words to articulate the trauma she had endured, but her eyes were clearly projecting into my mind the horror she had just endured.

I was placed there at the right time to provide her with an energy healing session in the hopes she would make it and thrive at the sanctuary. I sent her loving energy, gave her a vision of happiness frolicking in the pastures, and being a cow that has no worries in the world, where she would bond with the other residents, enjoy the sunshine and fresh hay, and be herself. I gave her reassurance that we would all be there to protect her, and we were all happy she had lived. This was her time to choose to take that opportunity to grow and love life in spite of how she was brought into this world.

She chose to live! She made it! With the love we all poured on her, she chose to live. She is happy, healthy, and connected with the other residents and the other volunteers who shower her with love and attention. I have her picture framed in my room to remind me of her on the days I don't see her. She has a special place in my heart because I was there to be part of the beginning of her journey in this life. Even though it was not the happiest and warmest entrance into this world, she has had the best experience from the moment she entered the sanctuary. This story always warms my heart beyond words.

HELEN, THE BLIND BISON

I lived in the Midwest for a while. My only experience with bison was visiting a wild safari where bison roamed free and came to the car windows to eat from our bucket full of feed. I remember how enormous their heads were, and I was quite intimidated by their size and how they found a way of getting through the car window to find the feed.

Fast forward quite a few years, I was visiting another sanctuary in Oregon that had rescued a blind bison. This animal was a remarkable story of love. She was born without eyesight and the farm owners did not want to keep her as this would mean—in their minds—more

PART 5: EXUDING HEALING ENERGY

work. Therefore, a loving lady decided to adopt the sweet baby to save her from slaughter. She raised her in her own home. For years, Helen lived with this lady who looked after her and cared for her like she would any other animal companion.

But one day, the caregiver had a car crash and was no longer capable of caring for Helen. It is not like she could hire a pet sitter to come and look after a bison! She had to let her go. Helen was brought to this sanctuary to be her new forever loving home. She was the only bison in the sanctuary. So, she had the whole pasture all to herself.

I would go into the pasture and sit down next to her to meditate for as long as she would allow me to. She would then lower herself to the ground and lie right next to me. Thinking back to my Midwest intimidating experience with bison, I was in awe at the fact I was comfortably sitting next to her without allowing fear to enter my mind.

As an animal healing energy practitioner, I also have a human mind I need to tame sometimes. This was one of those times.

I continued to visit Helen in the sanctuary, bringing her fruit. So chill and relaxed, I could tell she loved the company. She was social and wanted to be around other beings, animals and people alike, but she also loved her solitude. She grazed in the pasture peacefully, never pacing, never showing any signs of restlessness. She exuded contentment from those immense, gorgeous, brown eyes.

At some point I also took my Tibetan bowls and played for her. She enjoyed the sounds that raised her frequency and created a serene energetic space around her. She was very loved.

I also have a framed painting of Helen in my living room that I see multiple times every day, and the love I have for her has never faded. I love her today just as I loved her the day I met her. She passed recently of old age, and I always thank in my heart the lady who had the courage to raise her in her own home for all those years. Stories of humanity like this one are what make this world a better place.

She lived a full life and was deeply loved. She lived until she peacefully passed away in her sleep. I feel so fortunate I got to be part of her life. She, too, holds a very big, special place in my heart.

WHAT I LEARNED FROM THESE TWO STORIES OF CHARLOTTE AND HELEN

Energy healing works on the emotional body of the animals as well as their nervous systems. In spite of having different lives, both Charlotte and Helen had been removed from the opportunity of creating natural bonds with their biological mothers. This did not affect them negatively. The love they both received counteracted the effect of the trauma and allowed them to be happily content and at peace.

It is the invisible, intangible things that amaze me the most with energy healing. Even though my contribution was but a portion of the outpouring of unconditional love these animals received, I know deep in my core, they appreciated it immensely. Energy healing recalibrated the parts of their bodies affected by the experiences they had early in life. I feel so very honored to be of service to the animals.

I hope I have painted a clear picture of the practice I incorporated in my life to carry a higher frequency. Next, we can go over in detail the steps of the manual to happiness mentioned in my introduction. This is truly where we go, step by step, to transform our daily routine to a lifestyle that harnesses our superpower: unconditional love frequency. Are we ready to start? This is going to be truly transformational.

PART 6
LEADING A HEART-CENTERED LIFE

Today...

The gift of the present moment is here.
The promise of a new day...
A new beginning...
A new start...
The pain of yesterday stayed in the past,
And the worries of tomorrow have not yet arrived.
It is the gift of now!
It is a magical, yet ephemeral, time where the choice
is nobody else's but yours!
What experiences will fill this gift of the now?
Sadness...
Emptiness...
OR
Hope....

Peace....
Acceptance...
A glimmer of joy?

Or will it be an unstoppable wave of happiness washing away everything that brought you down?

Whatever it may be, it is for you to decide...
What does your heart say?
My wish for you is that you know, deep down...
The choice has always been and will always be yours!

So when I say, "Have a great day," it is a reminder to *choose* to have a great day. It is not simply a wish.

Happiness always comes from within... it is an inside job, not a random result of external circumstances.

STEPHANIE'S MANIFESTO

Many years ago, I sat down and wrote my manifesto, a written statement to document how I desire to carry out my life. This manifesto outlines my core values, my beliefs, what matters to me the most. It is not a to-do list of goals to be achieved. It is a written document that guides my thoughts and actions each day to keep me aligned with what drives me. Today, I would like to share it as an introduction to leading a heart-centered life.

Of course, this is what I aim to do in *my* life. It does not mean I am able and capable of doing it all 100 percent of the time. However, each day is a new beginning, and I start all over again. I look at it like each day is New Year's Day! I get up after falling, dust myself off, and I keep going.

STEPHANIE'S MANIFESTO

"Every day I will remind myself that happiness is a choice. I choose to not judge situations as good or bad; they just are what they are. It is always my choice to decide if I allow a situation to bring me down or not. It is always my choice. I am in control of how I choose to react.

I walk away from negative people and negative situations that cause me discomfort and unease. I choose to be surrounded only by people who love and care about me. It is my birthright to always feel loved.

I always do the right thing knowing that doing so is not always easy, but it is what will allow me to be happy with myself. My inner peace will allow me to sleep well every night.

I will always be careful where I decide to put my money. I will not support companies that destroy the environment and do not care for the highest and greatest good of the population. Nothing I buy is worth the cruelty, abuse, and total disrespect for the environment that certain companies practice.

I will eat mindfully with the purpose of nourishing my body for my greatest health. Eating is not a sport or activity to get me out of boredom or anxiety or anger, it is an activity to keep my body healthy so I can have a good life.

My natural state of being is happiness. If I am not happy, I will stop for a moment and ask myself mentally, What am I feeling now? The moment I identify it as anger, frustration, sadness, or disappointment, I will be able to do the necessary action to get back to my happy, natural state. This is a very simple question and such an effective technique to reset feelings.

Life is a series of lessons to be learned. The harder the situation, the more important the lesson. When I do not understand what the lesson is or what it is teaching me, then that situation is going to repeat again and again until I learn it. I need to be very self-aware and ask myself the question: What am I learning from this?

Friends come for a reason, a season, or a lifetime. I will not dwell in the sadness of seeing a friend go. There is always a purpose and there is always a reason. I will continue to be grateful for the moments I had with those friends, and I will open myself to receive new friends who bring more fun to my life.

Life is a gift: Every second, every minute, every hour, every day, is a gift to be enjoyed deeply. Wasting life on things that do not bring happiness is a crime. Life goes fast. Time flies and those moments will never come back. Every day, I decide to invest my time as if today is my last day. When I reach the end of my life, I will know each day was spent in the way that brought me the most happiness, and I will have no regrets.

I always speak my truth not with rudeness or with the intention of hurting anybody's feelings but to always express myself truthfully. Being true to myself is how I earn respect. Being true to myself is what really brings me inner peace. Speaking my truth is what allows me to be myself in this world. I live with no pretenses. I do not fake, and I don't try to be anything other than what I am.

I always put my best effort in everything I do, not because I want to be better than anybody else but because I am choosing to invest my precious time in those activities that are best for me. I will not invest my time in things done halfway—that would dishonor my own precious gift of time.

Every single day I choose to be kind to others just like I am kind to myself. Each being I encounter, a bird, a cat, a fly, a person, all have been created by divine universal intelligence, so who am I to disrespect them? They have the same right to be here as I do. I will always respect that and treat them with kindness. They are here fulfilling a divine life mission just like I am.

Every time I feel sad or disappointed in a situation, I will take the time to honor my feelings and grieve, then allow myself to have the emotion and let it go. I will not bottle up my feelings and repress them."

It is important to know that circumstances in life are not always what we expect, but we can always bring ourselves back to our natural happy state. Those moments of sadness and anger are there to teach us a lesson. What are we learning? That is the real question. We may know in the moment, perhaps. Or we will know after some time has passed. In the end, we will come out of it a wiser version of ourselves. That is what life is all about.

As an energy healing practitioner who continuously grows in the practice of different modalities of Reiki, I do set the intention to start each day with the traditional Reiki precepts.

Reiki Precepts

"Just for today, I will not anger.
Just for today, I will not worry.
Just for today, I will be grateful.
Just for today, I will do my work honestly.
Just for today, I will be kind to every living being"

Every day I will practice my self-care routine:

I will sleep enough hours to wake up rested.
I will drink water to let my body function properly.
I will do activities that bring me joy.
I will meditate at least thirty minutes a day to calm
the constant chatter in my mind.
I will pay it forward. I will do at least one act of
kindness for a friend or a stranger. Each time I smile,
I give the person a tiny piece of kindness. Who
knows? That may be the only act of kindness that
this person receives all day.

My hope with sharing my manifesto is to open the invitation for each of us to take inventory of what drives us in life, and perhaps invest a portion of our time writing our very own manifesto. Wouldn't it be a wonderful way of ensuring we are living our life in alignment with what fulfills us?

Let's take a moment to reflect on what fulfills us. That is a deep question.

Let's pause.

Breathe.

I hope we take the time to ponder on this for a moment.

MANUAL TO HAPPINESS

My first question when I became aware of the power of energy and the importance of staying balanced was, *How does one live a happier life? A more heart-centered life?*

Simple: Unlearn pretty much everything we think we know about life. Then, be still so we can listen to our hearts.

Again, simple, but not easy. This is perhaps the most difficult part of all. Once we unlearn, the rest is easy breezy! May these building blocks to a heart-centered life, based on the unconditional love frequency, open the door to inner happiness.

As the Dalai Lama says: **"Our sole purpose in life is to be happy."** At first glance, we may dismiss this statement as a utopian view on life. However, by now, we understand that not projecting our baggage on others requires serious self-awareness. It cannot be accomplished without discipline. It is not the result of luck. On the contrary. True happiness is the result of wisdom acquired through experience.

This manual provides the eleven steps to fulfill this job with more grace and less pain. We can learn the hard way or the easy way. I hope we all use this manual to learn the easier, less painful way. After all, it is our choice how we carry on in our lives.

I encourage us all to spend thirty days practicing each step to truly integrate these fundamental actions into our daily life. The results will be mind-blowing! This is roughly one year dedicated to spiritual growth, to personal enlightenment, and finally, to happiness. The brain needs a minimum of twenty-one consecutive days to solidify neurological pathways. Consistency and diligence is the key to success.

STEP 1: SELF-LOVE

I am working on becoming the happiest, most enlightened version of myself!

—Stephanie Stephan

Self-love means making the right choices to honor all parts of us: mind, body, feelings, emotions, and health!

We must cultivate self-love to get us through the hard times. Without self-love, we give up on ourselves because we mistakenly think we are not worth the effort. I am here to say: YES! We ARE worth the effort—every drop of blood and sweat that this entails. We are worth it, and we find ourselves once we go through it all. All we need is to put one foot in front of the other. Sometimes it can be a matter of days or weeks and sometimes months—perhaps years. But every single time we go through hard times, taking small steps can lead us to transformational changes.

We cannot give when our cup is empty. First, we need to have an overflowing cup ourselves, and then we are in a position where we can *make the choice* of helping others if we so wish. How can we even attempt to love our coworkers, our friends, our partners, our kids, our parents, or our family members when we have not learned to genuinely love ourselves first? Not loving ourselves first may lead to lack of healthy boundaries with the people in our closest circles. This may cause resentment if we feel like we have been taken advantage of, or we believe we have given too much, or we feel invisible or unappreciated. These situations often are the result of lack of healthy boundaries. When we love ourselves, we understand the importance of always enforcing these boundaries.

Self-love is not selfish. On planes we are instructed to put the oxygen mask on ourselves first before assisting others. In the next section we will cover concrete examples of self-love. Perhaps these examples will open up our minds to putting ourselves first so we can serve others. This is the opposite of what most of us have learned. This is one of the fundamental behaviors we need to unlearn.

FIRST EXAMPLE OF SELF-LOVE

We all look forward to our time off work at the end of a long workweek. How we choose to invest this precious time provides very good insight into how well we practice self-love. Here are three indicators of our self-love practice.

1—Prioritize Being Versus Doing

Let's manage time in a way that allows us to breathe, rest, and pause.

Pushing through the day leads to burnout. **We are human *beings* not human *doings*.** We need time to just be in order to thrive. Depriving ourselves of that intrinsic need is a recipe for failure in the long run. I know this from experience. I had always been the Energizer Bunny, going, going, *going* until I dropped. Pushing through the day is the equivalent of operating like a ticking bomb. It will explode in time. Without managing time well, we will burn out; it is not a question of if, it is a question of when.

2—Choose

Let's choose what brings us joy, not what will check off the obligations we committed to when we were not thinking clearly.

We live life with an endless list of tasks, errands, and more. But we have the choice to take time to decompress from it all. After all, we do not earn any gold stars for being the person who gets most done in one single day. What is this relentless urge to occupy every minute of our day? Where is our idle time to unwind, to just be? Let's choose to *be!*

3—Speak Our Truth

Often, we may overcommit because we say what we *believe* is expected from us. **Let's consider those people-pleasing days over, starting today.**

Self-care means putting ourselves first and others second. In the end, everyone benefits from that. We will be happy for speaking our truth; others will be happy because we are not resentful for doing what we did not want to do in the first place.

To practice self-love, we can start with micro-habits that are easy to make. For example, next time someone asks what we want for lunch, let's say what we want rather than leaving it up to the other person to choose on our behalf. Baby steps!

SECOND EXAMPLE OF SELF-LOVE

Let's imagine being at a family event, and the relatives are teasing us because of our choice of career. They are putting us down because they find it to be a funny topic of conversation. But deep down, we feel hurt and invalidated in our life choices.

Self-love encourages speaking our truth and establishing a boundary of respect toward self. We can start by stating that what is being said is not funny. Then follow that by saying, "Putting down a person due to their career choice is not amusing." We may also need to educate our family members about respect. We may add, "Respecting my choices means you are respecting me too; disrespecting my choices shows you don't respect me."

Establishing boundaries is practicing self-love, and this takes courage, but you are worth it.

PART 6: LEADING A HEART-CENTERED LIFE

THIRD EXAMPLE OF SELF-LOVE

Let's be in a relationship that fills our hearts.

One of the most soul-crushing experiences in life is living without love where one has to read between the lines to understand the message or has to walk on eggshells because someone is unable to self-regulate or lives in fear for a myriad of reasons. Staying in a marriage only out of duty for our children is another example. All of these scenarios show lack of self-love. To fully embrace the power of self-love, it is important to draw a plan of action to get out of the situation and end the relationship after ample attempts have been made without any success.

I personally would be miserable if I had chosen to stay married for my child's sake. It would have taken away the joy in my daily life. Whatever the situation, we need to always choose us, not the other person. If we don't choose us first, the choices we make will be in detriment of ourselves and those we are trying to protect. We can't give what we do not have.

FOURTH EXAMPLE OF SELF-LOVE

What we eat is a direct reflection of how much we value our health, our life, and ultimately our happiness. Do we eat junk food fully knowing the toxic effects it has on the body because we do not care about our health? Because ingesting substances that will cause us harm is not our concern at all?

Before doing anything, we ask ourselves, *Am I making a decision purely based on instant gratification?* If the answer is yes, chances are we could be sabotaging our happiness.

Self-love is making the right decision for long-term happiness, not instant gratification.

PRACTICE

Let's consider for the next thirty days pausing each time we are making a choice: attending the event, staying longer hours at work, showing up in a relationship, choosing what to eat, to watch, to listen to, etc.

Then let's ask these questions: Is this honoring my true desire? Am I honoring myself? Or am I going through the motions mindlessly because this is how it has always been?

We can rewire our brains to make ourselves a priority by making the right choices whether the decision we are making has small or much bigger consequences in our lives.

For additional ways to amplify our self-love practice, let's refer back to the Self-Love Guide in Part 4.

STEP 2: PRESENCE

The act of grounding ourselves through our senses is a powerful step towards cultivating presence. Rather than providing an explanation, I would love to open the invitation to join me in an imaginary walk in nature to experience presence together.

Grounding Ourselves in Nature

"Let's go for an extraordinarily mindful walk.
Let's feel the ground under our feet as it supports our bodies.
Let's notice how our feet make contact with the ground, as if each step is a kiss to Mother Earth.
Let's feel the gentle breeze softly brushing our skin.
Let's listen to the wind as it makes the leaves on the trees dance with rapture.
Let's observe with the curiosity of a child discovering

PART 6: LEADING A HEART-CENTERED LIFE

the world for the very first time!
Let's see the ladybug inconspicuously feeding on its favorite bugs or sweet nectar.
Let's look at the infinite diversity of shapes and textures of every leaf, tree, plant, and flower.
Let's take in their fragrances in the air!
Let's pay attention to the variety of scents!
What do our noses perceive? Is it the aromas of morning dew, or freshly bloomed flowers, or of chemical compounds being transmitted by the pines and evergreens? Or is it the sweet fragrance of the blades of grass the wind caresses on the open field?

Let's listen!
What does the wind say when it rustles the leaves of the trees next to us?
What do the squirrels, birds, and crickets say to us?
Let's marvel at the sun's rays permeating through the foliage, through the clouds.
Let's observe the light show that paints the sky and casts a golden hue on creation.
Let's feel!
Raindrops of life nourish the plants and our bodies.
What an exquisite feeling it is to feel raindrops as if we were kids again!
Let's taste!

Can we taste all this exuberance?
Presence is not just going for a walk; *presence is experiencing the entire wondrous universe in one single walk.*"

Eckhart Tolle explains presence very well in his book, *The Power of Now*. Cultivating awareness means experiencing the world through our senses and our hearts, not our minds.

We are more than a brain producing thoughts; we are more than a machine doing repetitive tasks every day. We are more than the memories of our life experiences. We are consciousness.

Cultivating awareness means bringing a sense of full presence in all we do. If we fail to practice presence, life will pass us by while we are prisoners of our mind.

The mind is a wonderful piece of art. It keeps us alive, learning steps to enable us to complete the same task easier and faster the next time we engage in it. Playing an instrument, operating a vehicle, finding directions to a location all get easier with repetition. The mind is fantastic and allows us to accomplish all of this.

There is a time and a place for everything: The heart is the center stage of life. It is the heart that builds connections, relationships, dreams, and desires that make life meaningful. The heart needs to be in charge in order to live a fulfilling existence. A mind in charge has no guardrails to keep us happy. Instead, a mind in control makes us feel like everything around us is out of control and forces us into a mental loop of anxiety and depression.

Cultivating awareness is bringing the heart back in charge of our lives—breaking free from the mental prison of our incessant thoughts. We do this by engaging our senses so the connection to our experience can keep us in the present moment and nowhere else. *That* is the key to cultivating awareness. We then have awareness of our feelings and our emotions. That is when we are truly free from our self-inflicted prison.

PART 6: LEADING A HEART-CENTERED LIFE

FIRST EXAMPLE OF PRESENCE

Let's say we are washing the dishes. To bring more presence in, we focus on the temperature of the water running through our fingers. We feel the solidity of the pan we are currently washing. We focus on the feeling of the bubbles of the detergent as it creates mini bursts of air in our hands. We then take a deep breath and inhale the aroma of roses from the dishwasher soap scent. We notice and pay attention to the light coming from our kitchen window and how it is shining directly on the rest of the dishes we are about to wash. Our body is fully engaged in the act of washing dishes.

When we are fully in the moment, all our senses are engaged in this experience, right here, right now at its fullest. Our minds do not wander. There are no thoughts, only sensations. We are in a state of joy as we take in this wet, warm, and aromatic experience of washing dishes. For as long as we are washing the dishes and cultivating presence, our mind is resting. When we are done with the dishes, we feel energized. We just experienced pure presence. During this time, we may sense what our hearts are feeling; there may be a sense of pleasure of just being. Our full attention was on how we felt in the moment by engaging all our senses. Presence is very effective in getting us out of the mental activity in our minds and into the feeling of our hearts.

SECOND EXAMPLE OF PRESENCE

Let's say we are at work where we interact with many other people. While they are talking to us on any given topic on any given day, we are rehearsing in our minds all we want to say before they are even done talking. We aren't listening; we aren't even mentally there. This is an example of lack of presence.

This is a very common reason we don't communicate well with others. Miscommunication happens, misunderstandings happen, assumptions are made. We fail to be fully present, and our communications fail as a result.

PRACTICE

What if for the next thirty days, we make a commitment to ourselves to be present while communicating with others. Let's avoid preparing what we are going to say while the other person is speaking. Instead, let's follow these steps:

1. Let's listen to understand, not to respond
2. Let's capture the idea clearly
3. Let's repeat what we heard to make sure we got it right
4. Let's ask the person for a moment to run through the information they just provided
5. Let's pause to formulate what we want to say in response
6. Finally, we can share our opinion on what was said

This practice is magical. Presence is a game changer in interpersonal communications.

In thirty days, we will be able to retrain our brain to be present while others speak. If others emulate us, they will then, in return, be fully present while we speak to them too. The beauty of cultivating presence is that we are giving the other person the best gift we can give another: our undivided attention. This is another flavor of unconditional love. In a world of multi-tasking and endless distractions, imagine how good it feels to have someone's complete, undivided attention!

I encourage us all to journal at the end of the thirty-day practice to track the changes we have been able to see by shifting focus and response after listening to others.

What has this practice taught us about others that we did not know before?

What did this practice teach us about ourselves that we didn't know before?

STEP 3: DETACHMENT - WE ARE NOT OUR ROLES

I would like to mention again Eckhart Tolle from whom I learned I am not the role I play in this life. Here is how I translated his teachings into my personal experience.

I play the role of mother. But I am not a mother.

I play the role of a student. But I am not a student.

I play the role of a friend. But I am not a friend.

I play the role of a neighbor, but I am not a neighbor.

I play the role of a granddaughter, but I am not a granddaughter.

If roles in life do not define my identity, then who am I?

That is really the question to ponder to reach a higher understanding of the essence of our existence.

If we are not any of these, it is because we are *more* than the sum of all of these roles put together.

We are awareness itself.

We are consciousness.

We are the silent observer, watching our own life unfold as it unfolds.

We are presence.

This presence is there regardless of whether we choose to play the role of a student or not.

Awareness exists whether we choose to play the role of a friend or not.

Consciousness is there whether we are awake or asleep, whether we are alive or have departed.

In our core, we have no label, we are Oneness. If a role changes in our life, we create another role. We are still ourselves regardless of the role we choose to have in any given moment.

If we are no longer a student, we still are ourselves.

If we are no longer a neighbor, we still are ourselves.

If we are no longer a granddaughter, we still are ourselves.

Understanding the difference of what we are in our core and what roles we choose to play in life is one of the most liberating truths there is.

Knowing we are conscious awareness and not a role is expansive.

Knowing we are presence, and we are not reduced to a label in life, is magnificent.

If we ever have struggled with the questions of who am I? and who do I want to become? the answer is simple: We are conscious awareness, and we deep down have the desire to be love in physical form.

This is a very profound truth that I wish was common knowledge so all of us could embrace the divine essence connecting us to God, to Source, to It All. We collectively represent a little piece in the puzzle that all together makes up this infinite Oneness.

PRACTICE

Let's practice detachment from our roles. Each morning let's say this out loud: **I AM. I AM love. I AM awareness. I AM consciousness. I AM.**

Saying this to ourselves in front of the mirror while we look directly into our eyes and understand in our hearts the truth of this statement will transform our lives forever. It sounds so simple, perhaps even silly. However, the profound benefits of this practice unfold over time. It took me by surprise how this changed me to my core. Our identity goes far beyond our roles. Taking the time to remind ourselves of this truth daily anchors it into our being. We will begin to walk through life with this knowledge and feel far less attached to our roles.

We are still embodying those roles, and they still bring us a sense of fulfillment, but the difference is they no longer dictate how we feel about our self-worth or our overall happiness. We are worthy regardless of the roles we choose to play at any stage in our lives. We are worthy because we are awareness itself and knowing that is one of the most fundamental reasons of happiness. It is not something we can ever, ever lose.

I invite us all to journal this practice and write down how we feel at the end of the thirty days. Have we acquired a new sense of detachment from the roles we play? Is there a sense of liberation from these labels?

STEP 4: SHIFTING PERSPECTIVES - FROM VICTIMHOOD TO EMPOWERMENT, FROM LACK TO ABUNDANCE

Once we have internalized in our being the truth of who we are in essence, let's shift perspectives.

Our perspectives prior to this practice are very much anchored in the roles we play. Now we are building a wider and different perspective of life and how we interact with others.

Victimhood is a common theme among those who have yet to learn their true, divine essence. I imagine we have all been there. Thoughts of *why me?* Or why did this happen *to me?*

Let's say a person wrongs us, a situation is negative, an unexpected outcome shocks us, and each of these situations is devastating. Or are they?

The best example of shifting perspectives is a story an artist told me one day as I was visiting a metaphysical fair in Portland.

His painting was the portrait of a young man and his horse in what seemed to be a ranch nestled in a bucolic landscape. What caught my attention was the horse of course. I tend to be drawn to animals even in paintings. However, the artist pointed out the presence of the young man. At that point I noticed there was also an older man in the painting. He asked me if I knew the story about this scene and I replied, no. I just assumed it was a Western scene and I was simply admiring the beautiful representation of the horse.

He then proceeded to tell me. It was a story of a ranch owner who had a son. His son loved his horse and took pride in training and riding him everyday. The friends in town would say to the rancher, "What a great thing that your son loves horses." The rancher would respond, "It is not good, it is not bad, it just is." Then one day the son fell off the horse and broke a leg. He had to wear a cast for a long time, during which time the townspeople would comment, "Oh what a bad thing just happened to your son; we are sorry." The rancher would reply, "It is not good, it is not bad, it just is."

The townspeople were perplexed at his answers and wondered, *Is he not able to see what a tragedy has just happened to his son?* Then a war started and all the young men in the town were asked to enlist in the military. But not the rancher's son, because he was injured from the fall. Then the people told the rancher, "You are so lucky your son did not have to go to war." And you can guess what the rancher responded one more time…

The moral of the story is that all of life is a matter of perspective. We do not know what we do not know. It is best to not place labels of judgment as good or bad, but to allow things to just be. Situations just are. We have learned to make then positive or negative depending on the label we choose to place on them. Let's consider taking a stance of neutrality. In other words, let's consider unlearning the stance of duality. No, things are not inherently all good or all bad. This is a mindset that leads to unhappiness. There is an entire range of gray. Nothing is all black, and nothing is all white. Can we learn to enjoy the plethora of gray where life resides? Can we learn to use no labels? Cast no judgments? Can we be more like the rancher in this story?

This chat with the artist happened many moons ago and I have vividly recorded it in my psyche to remind me to stay clear of labels. It helps me avoid judgment. Of course, I have moments when I revert back to labels. However, each day is a new beginning, remember? This is my philosophy, and I do not beat myself up if I start all over again the next day. After all, I am learning, and I give myself grace.

Another pivotal moment in my life that made me rethink my perspective on victimhood for good was the book called *Your Soul's Plan* by Robert Schwartz. This book includes stories of indescribable hardships and how, as he connected to the higher souls of regression patients, he got to witness the conversations that took place as each of these souls planned their lives before being born. If this sounds a little out there, remember, we do not cease to exist because we are energy and energy does not disappear, it only transforms itself. A dying soul is an impossibility.

The stories in Schwartz's book explained in detail the reason hardships were chosen. Each would bring about a very transformational change in the person's soul, the person's soul group, and the humanity around this soul.

For example, let's consider the story of a person who is unhoused. Why might they have chosen this? It is an act of bravery. This soul chose to be an example to teach others kindness.

Another story Schwartz included was about a person who suffered severe injuries as a result of a bomb. This soul chose to be injured in this way in order to learn forgiveness, and he is therefore an example of forgiveness to others.

There are many wonderful stories in his book and what I learned from reading them is that things are not what we think they are. **We are not victims of circumstances**. We have certain missions we choose before our birth in order to collectively advance in our consciousness. We cocreate the rest of our lives based on the choices we make. However, our missions were carefully planned before we were born. Therefore, even the most unspeakable acts have a deeper meaning. They did not happen by chance. Life is a divine orchestration of events that lead to something far more meaningful than what our minds can comprehend.

Consider one of the most horrific times in our modern history, World War II. What was the outcome of this horror? For the first time, the world came together and created the United Nations Organization, which had a mission of keeping the harmony among countries, continents, and people for world peace. Stories of humanity, kindness, endurance, and ineffable emotional strength came to inspire the rest of the world that yes, in spite of the horror, life is worth living. Even in these extreme circumstances, there is a light shining through the darkness to show us the way, if only we shift perspectives from the obvious to the not so obvious. I personally cannot comprehend the crimes against humanity perpetrated during this war. I do not condone this war, or any war for that matter. However, I do see that humanity did unite after the war was over to help promote peace among nations for the first time in modern history.

SHIFTING PERSPECTIVES FROM LACK TO ABUNDANCE

This one is one of the most beautiful, profound, and heart-opening practices I have incorporated in my daily life.

When we were in school—generation Z or older—chances are all our tests were corrected in red ink. All the things we had done wrong were highlighted in red. Our very impressionable, sensitive hearts and brains were trained to only focus on what had been missed, what was incorrect, what was not the expected answer. We did not see our tests for their whole value; all the red on our papers directed our attention only to the wrong answers, not the right ones. This happened week after week, month after month, year after year, for all our grade school years and beyond. By the time we graduated at eighteen, we had been very effectively trained to only focus on the negative.

We applied this to our lives and to all we did. We have it very ingrained in our mindset. It is our programming.

We may have it all, but we will inevitably only focus on that *one* thing we believe is missing and we will make ourselves unhappy obsessing over that one thing and one thing only. If only I had *that* job, I would be happy. If only I had *that* spouse, I would be happy. If only I had *that* kid, I would be happy. By having the mindset we learned in school, we negate the other millions of things we already have which already give us happiness. Our programming runs in our subconscious mind and sabotages our happiness on a daily basis.

What if we were to shift perspectives and focus on all that we *do* have?

First of all, we have life. We woke up today. We already are incredibly fortunate as many did not wake up today.

Second, we can breathe. The breath filling our lungs with oxygen is not to be taken for granted. Remember the days when we could not breathe freely, and we had to always wear masks? Or the days of fires when the air was toxic, and we could not breathe freely without causing damage to our lungs? Breathing is a gift. Let's always remember how important breathing is because it sustains our life on this planet.

Third, chances are we woke up in a bed with a roof over our head. Let's remember this is not something everyone can say. Regardless of anything else about our house—the size, the age of construction, the color, the taxes, anything, regardless of all of that—at the end of the day, we have one. We can then focus on what we *do* have—the house—and not on what the house may be missing that is causing us angst.

Fourth, we are loved. We have family, friends, neighbors, and community. We already have an abundance of love all around us constantly showering us with unconditional loving energy, refueling our hearts, uplifting us, encouraging us, and making us feel a deep connection. That is priceless. Love does not have to come from one person. We are already getting it from multiple sources in multiple ways at multiple times and oh-so-many scenarios. What if we take a moment to acknowledge the abundance of love that is constantly coming our way instead of focusing on the significant other we believe is missing in our lives? Isn't obsessing over that *one* person we think we are missing in our lives negating the abundance of love we are already receiving from everyone else?

And the list continues....

PRACTICE

I invite us all for thirty days to practice shifting perspectives and unlearning all those things that do not serve us anymore. Shift from victimhood to empowerment. What is the lesson of our hardship? How will that lesson serve us to have a happier life? Can we try to come up with at least ten things we already have before we even start our day—not material things, intangible things. The ones that truly matter. How about we give ourselves ten to fifteen minutes of intentional brainstorming on this topic?

Then we can write in our journal how we feel about life now that we have shifted perspectives to take charge of our happiness. Chances are, it will be an eye-opening exercise, and we may never want to go back to the way we used to think. Staying with it is the key to happiness. Unlearning what we learned for over a decade of life requires diligent repetition. New ways of thinking need to be repeated consistently with conscientious effort before they can become the default way of thinking.

STEP 5: ACCEPTANCE: FOCUS ON WHAT WE CAN DO

Mother Teresa of Calcutta was a very inspirational humanitarian. She used to say: **"I alone cannot change the world, but I can cast a stone across the waters to create many ripples."**

Gandhi used to say: **"Be the change you want to see in the world."**

These are very inspirational leaders who changed nations, who changed humanity, and were each only one person. What if Mother Teresa had stopped herself from being a humanitarian just because when she began, she felt overwhelmed about facing the poverty numbers in her country alone? She would not have even started the movement she created for thousands to follow.

What if Gandhi had stopped himself from dreaming of change for his country? Quite possibly India would not be free today.

What do these two remarkable people have in common?

They did not focus on the problem itself; instead, they focused all their attention and energy on what they could do toward the solution. That is the key to happiness.

Do we get bogged down by the state of affairs in the world and allow the news to make us feel defeated, hopeless, lost, and depressed? Or do we turn off the news and use that time to participate in the solution instead?

For example, if we worry about a specific candidate winning an election, one way we can contribute toward the solution is to stop supporting those bigger conglomerates who fund their campaigns. We can choose to not buy their products. That is something we have full control over; why not use our economic power?

What about the environment? We are told about climate change having cataclysmic effects in multiple countries, but how many times have we seen environmental solutions being advertised on TV? They are not. We need to intentionally search for them. They exist. They are there! There are many organizations implementing effective solutions already. How about instead of being pulled into the fear of the problem, we direct our precious energy toward getting engaged in the solution? Why not amplify these organizations' voices? We can direct our economic power towards those companies that support them already instead.

The power is in the numbers and the numbers increase one at a time to collectively make incredible change happen. Let's never underestimate the incredible change ignited with just one single person. Let's never underestimate the undeniable progress one person can do.

Inaction perpetuates the problem. What if we are that one person that initiates the action that will inspire others to follow. What if we try?

When shifting focus from the problem toward the solution, we feel empowered to create a change in the world, and it often starts locally. We may not change what happens in every country, but if we contribute to change that happens in our own neighborhood, we are compounding a positive accumulative effect. In the book called *Micro Habits: Small Changes - Big Results* by Ron Kness, the author highlights the undeniable power of small, consistent effort. After reading the book, it's easy to see how small daily progress over time makes the most transformational changes possible.

What happens in cases where things are outside of our control? For example, a family member who is doing drugs, our workplace having layoffs, or a health diagnosis that is less than desirable can leave us feeling helpless. The same concept of focusing on the solution applies here.

We cannot change others; we can only be there to provide support and show them love so they learn to love themselves enough to want to change their lives. Practicing acceptance of this truth frees us from the burden of trying in vain to force them to change their ways. We each are given life and we each choose to live it our way. **We do not live through somebody else's life in the same way that others do not live their lives through ours. It is called sovereignty.** The key here is knowing when to accept what is while providing nonjudgmental love to the person making choices we would not make for ourselves. I learned this lesson the hard way, but I am happier now I know not to carry the insurmountable burden of trying to change a loved one's life. I can only change my own. Acceptance. It is not easy, but it is possible.

FIRST EXAMPLE OF ACCEPTANCE

My daughter was genetically predisposed to mental illness due to her dad's mental illness. The trigger for his psychosis was recreational drugs. I had warned my daughter before college not to do drugs not only because of the unforgiving effects they will have long term, but also because she ran the risk of triggering in her brain a similar psychotic event as her dad's.

My advice fell on deaf ears. The consequence was devastating. She suffered from multiple psychotic events. I managed to get through those difficult times and somewhat keep my own sanity through the practice of acceptance. Each day I would remind myself to accept this has happened and to remember that it is out of my control. Acknowledging this fact does not solve the problem but helped me remain calmer. In return, acceptance allowed me to take a far less reactive stance towards the situation. **With a clear mind come better decisions and with better decisions come better choices**. Acceptance has that positive ripple effect.

I am sharing this example with the intent of destigmatizing the topic of mental health. The brain is another organ in our physical body which is susceptible to disease. I don't see anybody being shamed for having genetic heart disease or kidney disease or lung disease. For this reason, I don't understand the logic behind stigmatizing brain disease. It is an organ in the body. Shaming those with mental illness is as illogical to me as shaming someone for having heart disease or kidney disease. I hope this example can open the door to looking at mental health from this other perspective. A more compassionate one.

SECOND EXAMPLE OF ACCEPTANCE

What about layoffs at work? We discussed earlier how roles can change but we still are who we are. When layoffs are coming, we can take charge by preparing instead of adopting a victimhood mentality. We can choose to stand in our power; and we can plan our strategy in order to be ready to find another job elsewhere. These may include more aligned choices to what we want to accomplish in our career. Even in a scenario like this, we still have a way of taking charge to bring into our reality a most desirable outcome. Proactivity is the name of the game when it comes to a situation involving layoffs.

THIRD EXAMPLE OF ACCEPTANCE

What if there is a health diagnosis that is less than promising? We know that what we eat impacts our health. Our bodies remake themselves every seven years with the nutrients we ingest. We have the ability to change our DNA based on the choices we make each day. These facts remind us that nothing is written in stone. A change in the course of a diagnosis is always possible. Spontaneous remission is a phenomenon where a disease such as cancer disappears without medical intervention. When focusing on what we *can* change, we can change our lifestyle. We can then give the body the ability to regenerate itself and come back to homeostasis again. We have a lot we have control over. Our health included. Let's use our mindset to lead the way towards the proper action. Changes do happen. There is always the possibility of bringing a positive change by focusing our intention on the solution instead of the problem. Joe Dispenza wrote extensively on this subject. He is living proof that we can revert our body back to homeostasis. I highly recommend reading his book *Becoming Supernatural* to understand this superpower we all have dormant in our hearts.

EDDY THE BETTA FISH

Here is a short story of a moment when the departure of an animal companion was inevitable. Even though we do not have control of the outcome, we do have control over how we choose to handle the outcome.

My daughter had a betta fish named Eddy. Eddy was in his last few days of life. He had already been with her for a couple of years, and it was time to depart.

As an animal energy healing practitioner, I wanted to provide Eddy with a smooth transition to the other side. I proceeded to hold his vase and offer unconditional love frequency. I did this each day for a few minutes. To my surprise, instead of passing peacefully, Eddy chose to live for another month before he finally departed.

Perhaps a fish this tiny may not sound like an animal companion to some. But he was a companion indeed. He shared his stunning beauty every day for us to admire. He interacted with us as we moved around the room, and he wanted to follow along with us from his small vase. There was clearly a connection between my daughter and Eddy.

WHAT I LEARNED FROM THIS STORY

No animal is too small to benefit from unconditional loving energy. Let's allow them to surprise us with what they will do with the energy we shower on them.

PRACTICE

For the next thirty days, I invite us all to take a look at our life and then pick a situation that is bothering us about our life or about the world. Then identify what solution we can focus on to bring positive change to the situation. Write down at the end of the thirty days how we feel about the situation after having taken positive action toward it. Perhaps it is resolved, perhaps it is not, but the most important thing is how we *feel* about it. Have we gone from feeling hopeless to feeling more hopeful? Have we gone from feeling defeated to feeling empowered? Humans experience a range of emotions; have ours changed or has their intensity decreased? Journaling will help us see this transformation.

STEP 6: PRACTICING GRATITUDE

Gratitude

"I steep tea in a cup.
I am grateful for that exquisite aroma of leaves and
citrus emanating from it.
I am grateful my hands can feel the warmth from

PART 6: LEADING A HEART-CENTERED LIFE

that hot cup of tea.
I am grateful for the farmers who picked each leaf of
tea that made this experience possible for me.
I am grateful for the soil that nourished the tea
plants.
I am grateful for the sun, the rain, and the wind that
brought life to these plants.
I am grateful for all the workers who made it possible
for me to have this tea in my cup today.
And I take the first sip.
I am grateful I am alive.
I get to enjoy this tea.
To many, this may be a simple pleasure, but
To me, it is an expression of being alive.
I am grateful I am alive so I can have this cup of tea!
A happy life is nothing but a series of those little
things that warm our hearts and our soul."

—Stephanie

I mentioned earlier that as I built my happiness practice, I worked on gratitude. I believe this is one of the most transformational practices to effectively shift our perspective to see the world in a whole different light. It allows us to see events and circumstances in a new way and to have a deeper appreciation for this journey we call life.

I love to lead a gratitude meditation, and I can pick quite literally anything and go into detail on how this one item is something I am deeply grateful for. It is a skill I developed through daily intentionality.

STEPHANIE STEPHAN

FIRST EXAMPLE OF GRATITUDE

Let's say we are drinking a cup of tea. It is one of the most comforting things I experience every day. Every cell in my body bursts into joy with every sip of tea I take. Honestly! This is how I practice gratitude with tea. But it could be anything we love. We can follow the same steps.

As I hold the cup of hot tea in my hands, I engage all my senses in this magnificently pleasant experience. I feel the heat from the cup warm up my typically cold hands. I am grateful for the heat element of my cup. The skin on my hands, my muscles, and my joints all feel soothed in the warmth of the cup of tea. My body feels grateful, and I have not even taken my first sip.

Then I take in the aroma emanating from the cup in wisps of steam that dance in the air in front of me. I am grateful for this visual invitation! At the same time my nostrils take in the wonderful smell of the tea, I am instantly transported back to previous times and moments when I smelled this same aroma and the joy I felt. I am grateful for that.

I look into the cup, and I see the color of my tea, which takes me to the process of harvesting, preparing, packing, and transporting the tea. *How did it go from being a green leaf on a tea plant to being almost black in my cup?* I wonder. I am grateful for every single person who chose to work in the tea industry in all the steps of the making of the tea that allowed me to have this exact cup in my hands.

Had it not been for each of the farm workers doing their jobs, I would not have this joyful experience. I remember the sound of the water boiling as my mouth starts watering in anticipation. I am grateful because I have the electric power to boil water for this tea. Without heat, drinking hot tea would not be possible. I am thankful for the electricity generated by the Earth, then brought into my home, and I am deeply grateful I am financially able to afford it. All these factors had to play out for me to enjoy this cup of tea.

I take my first sip of tea and the pleasure it brings to my taste buds is indescribable. I feel the tea warm my body and it's like receiving the most loving hug from the person you love the most in the world. I close my eyes and take in the moment. All my senses are fully engaged, present. I am in a pure state of joy. I am grateful for being alive so I can enjoy this pleasurable experience of drinking a cup of tea.

I recently went to an organic herbal farm in Southern Oregon. I saw for the first time the plant used in earl grey tea. I was so grateful to meet this plant in person for the first time in my life that I, in fact, had tears in my eyes as I stood in front of this field. I had a moment of silence in front of these plants which represented the number of times I had been so happy drinking a cup of their tea. I felt I had met a person I had loved my entire life, a person who had made my life happy, and I finally stood in front of this person to mentally say, *Thank you for your service.*

I don't remember ever becoming this emotional when meeting a plant for the first time. This one, because of my relationship with tea, brought tears of deep gratitude to my eyes.

This is how I practice gratitude. I always drink tea with a smile. I am feeling an immense sense of gratitude without the need to utter any words. The joy is felt in my heart.

Gratitude can be practiced with pleasant situations but is it possible to practice it when we encounter unpleasant situations too?

SECOND EXAMPLE OF GRATITUDE

Years back I had a bicycle accident. I lost consciousness and woke up in the ER surrounded by half a dozen of my cycling friends. I had broken my left clavicle and was in a lot of pain. I had to have surgery because the triple fracture was severe and would not heal well on its own.

I remember one of these dear friends coming to visit me as I was recovering from surgery at home. He was very pleasantly surprised to see me in such good spirits, and he made a comment regarding how happy he was to see me like that. He had expected things to be different, to which I replied, "I am so very grateful I did not die in that accident. I could have broken my skull and had irreparable damage to my brain, but my helmet protected me, and my head is OK. I am grateful I did not lose my eyesight. My sunglasses took a beating when I hit the ground but did not break, keeping my eyes safe. Also, I am grateful all I need is time to recover from surgery and after this I will resume my life as it was before the accident. I did not lose mobility, and I am still here to continue raising my daughter and enjoying her childhood."

Again, it is all a matter of perspective. I healed extremely fast; my doctor was quite surprised. I healed at the rate of a professional athlete. My body responded quite well to my hopeful outlook on life. I was also very grateful for that fast recovery. My circle of friends was part of why I recovered so fast. They showered me with lots of tender loving care and I felt very loved.

Many would have been devastated by having an accident. Let's be honest. Who wants to be in an accident? Nobody does. However, once we are in one, can we pay attention to all the factors that made it possible for us to survive it? Isn't that something for which to be grateful? As I always tell my daughter, "Things can always be worse; be grateful they are not." Having this as a reminder allows me to always shift my attention to all the benefits of a situation at present compared to what could have been.

Another gratitude practice I do when I wake up is go outside to walk my dog. I am grateful for the new day, for the smell of the air, the different plants, the different trees, the color of the sky, and the majestic display of rays at sunrise that always leave me in awe. I am grateful the trees provide shade in the summer and oxygen for me to breathe fresh air every day. I am grateful for the song of the birds uplifting me with their beautiful frequencies of love. I am grateful I have a body able to take me on this walk and senses to take it all in. I am grateful my dog loves the walks and grateful I get to take him out every day and see the change of the seasons, day by day, week by week, month by month.

Every day is different in very subtle ways, and every day the experience of having the energy, health, body, time, and proximity to the woods to make this walk possible is a constant act of gratitude for me. I get to stop often and admire the beautiful colors of the trees, the beauty of the flowers, the inviting sound of the wind rustling in the leaves, the warmth of the sun's rays as they touch my face and warm up my back. It is all an orchestration of joyful moments that collectively make my walk a happy experience. I am grateful for every single one of these moments. I am present. I take it all in. They invigorate me. My day starts with serenity and admiration.

By the time I am back home from the walk and ready to start the day, my outlook on life is full of hope and joy because I was just given a wonderful moment communing with the exquisite beauty of nature. I am recharged.

When we live in a constant state of gratitude, there is little room for anxiety, depression, or other disorders that afflict our minds. We give our minds rest. We live life by connecting to the world around us through our senses instead of processing the world around us through our mental processes. The mind then is trained to stay quiet while the senses are at work absorbing all the external stimuli. The happiest way to live is by practicing gratitude and never taking anything in our experience for granted.

Those daily moments we may not pay attention to are, in fact, quite magical. They deserve our admiration. The birds may choose to sing elsewhere, or the trees may choose not to thrive. The wind may blow in a different direction changing the landscape completely. The flowers may not bloom if they no longer get the nutrients they need from the soil. Things could be different. But they aren't. Each of them chose to be there in our surroundings, and their presence in turn, enhances our life experience. It's not something to take for granted, is it? It is quite an orchestration of wondrous marvels that make up the natural scene in front of our eyes. It is up to us to notice.

PRACTICE

Now it is our turn. I invite us all to give it a try. For thirty days, let's practice this type of gratitude for two different things. Consider choosing one thing we love—this will be the warmup to establish the habit of actively and consciously paying attention through the senses to be in a state of gratitude. Once we have built that muscle, let's think about choosing a second thing, something we do not like as much, and find a way of seeing it from a more positive perspective. We can identify those silver linings and feel gratitude for them.

At the end of the thirty days, we can then journal what we observed. What has changed? Is it a calmer mind and grateful heart that makes us feel content for longer periods in the day? Could it be a shift of perspective toward life in general? What shifted for us? Paying attention to the subtle changes opens the door for bigger changes to take place. It all starts with baby steps.

STEP 7: PRACTICING EMPATHY

"The highest form of knowledge is empathy, for it requires us to suspend our egos and live in another's world."

—Plato

Alfred Adler, a psychiatrist, eloquently said that empathy is **"Seeing with the eyes of another, listening with the ears of another, and feeling with the heart of another."**

Compassion and empathy are both wonderful qualities; however, they are not the same.

Compassion is feeling kindness toward the suffering of another.

Empathy is *feeling* the suffering of another.

In this section, we delve into empathy. It was empathy that helped open my heart exponentially in a short period of time. Recent publications on the topic of emotional intelligence cover empathy in great detail and provide many tools to learn to develop it. It is no wonder that many consider empathy to be the highest form of emotional intelligence. It means understanding one's feelings and emotions so well that we can also put ourselves in another person's shoes and understand their feelings and emotions too.

This is very likely the most difficult of all the building blocks in my manual to happiness. We are trained to be in our minds all the time and to think only about ourselves, so empathy is a skill to cultivate and consciously practice. This is particularly true in individualistic cultures. Not so much in community-driven cultures.

Let's go over some examples on how to uncover this fascinating world of feeling what another person feels.

This is how I learned it. Perhaps this will provide some helpful guidance.

FIRST EXAMPLE OF EMPATHY

Once a day, I worked for an hour on imagining the person in front of me was *me* but in another body, in another life, with another set of experiences, and with another age and mindset. This requires an incredibly vivid imagination. I often passed someone on my way to the cafeteria and I would say to myself, *That person is me, taller, having different thoughts, perhaps having different worries than me, but that person and I are the same. We both have hearts that hold the frequency of unconditional love.*

I would go on… imagining each person I encountered was in fact me. *We are the same. We have the same Divine Essence, Prana energy, Chi, or Holy Spirit I hold in my heart. That person is me with a different background, different upbringing, different school, and different perspective of life. But we are the same. We both have the spark of light that makes our hearts beat, our organs function, and brings life to our bodies.*

Then I would run into someone at the grocery store, and I would follow the same method. I held the awareness of how the external looks are different, yes, but the heart still beats, the spark of energy is in the heart, and the divine essence is there. Just like me.

I sometimes was met with a look or comment from someone who happened to be frazzled at the moment, but again, I would follow the same method because I have days when I feel frazzled too. That person is still me. I then imagined all the reasons I may feel frazzled. Then, I was able to meet this person with grace. That person is me, frazzled just like I am too sometimes.

I thought of the days when the alarm did not go off and I woke up late and had to hurry to get to work on time, or a moment when what I expected would happen did *not* happen. I had moments of feeling frazzled, struggling to still make it work in spite of everything going on in my personal life.

Then I would mentally go back to the person who was frazzled when they made a comment to me or gave me a look, and I would imagine how they felt in the moment and how it was similar to how I have felt when my alarm did not go off on time. In moments like these, there is an understanding that we are human, and we go through a vast range of emotions when situations do not go our way, especially when we have not developed techniques to self-regulate.

I also imagined, while driving, seeing a driver recklessly approach my car, swerve, and almost hit me as they quickly sped up and continued endangering other drivers on the road. I imagined what circumstances this person could be going through to make them behave in such a precarious way. Did the driver receive a call that his wife is in the hospital, and it may be minutes before she passes away urging him to absolutely get there on time? Is it because this person just recently got laid off, tried to numb his feelings with substances, and this driving is the aftermath of a poor decision? I do not know the answer. I do know there is a reason.

I then try to remember, if there ever was a time when I acted recklessly in any way, driving or not, because I was going through a difficult time or got news about a loved one. Chances are, yes, more than once I did something reckless. My judgment would have been clouded because of fear, despair, anger, or other emotions I could not control in that moment. With this knowledge, instead of automatically casting judgment toward that driver as if I was any better than him, I would empathize with him. Because I understand whatever he is going through is not easy, and this recklessness is saying, *I feel out of control.*

It doesn't mean I know exactly what another feels. Empathy means I can put myself in their shoes and understand it is not easy for them. I will not feel exactly the same because I am not that person. But I can imagine the feeling. I can relate. As a result, I can be less judgmental and practice more grace toward them in that moment.

Practicing empathy happened over time for me. I did not always know what the other person or the animal felt. But setting the intention that I wanted to learn, I wanted to understand—in addition to paying attention to their suffering—opened my heart to empathy. Today, if someone is going through a rough time and they are telling me their story, I inevitably tear up. Before my energy healing practice, I would listen to them, but I would not tear up as a result. Something in my heart shifted. I am more open to feeling what others are feeling.

Here are a couple of examples where I realized I had become more empathetic but also more empathic. It was an intellectual understanding of what another is going through but also experiencing the feeling as if it was me going through that situation too.

SECOND EXAMPLE OF EMPATHY

I visited the animals at the sanctuary and heard the reports on how everyone was doing. As the person telling me the news engaged in conversation with me, I started sensing the deep feelings she had for each of the animals in the sanctuary. I sensed her concern for their well-being and for their health. I teared up because it was my heart listening to her deep concern; it was no longer the words that I was listening to. My heart was feeling the emotions carried by the sound of her words.

THIRD EXAMPLE OF EMPATHY

Another way I practice empathy is to always put myself in the shoes of another. I remember one day my coworkers were starting to tease another coworker who forgot to mute himself in a call and we all heard him getting upset at a driver on the way to work. Everyone thought it was funny to pick on him. But for me, it was not OK to laugh at the expense of another person, because I have been in his shoes, and I do not like getting my feelings hurt when I make a mistake. It may be common practice in certain workplace cultures; however, I do not endorse it.

I spoke up and asked my coworkers, "Who here has not done this before?" It was not to sound like a mom scolding a kid, but an opportunity for everyone to shift their perspective and turn the situation back on themselves and practice empathy. I was not surprised at all when everyone stopped laughing and the phone line went dead silent. Suddenly, they had been reminded that they had done the same at one time or another.

Empathy does not require us to have lived exactly the same situation the other person has lived to understand their pain. Empathy is simply asking, *How would this be for me if I had to face a challenging moment like this under their circumstances? Not my circumstances, theirs.*

FOURTH EXAMPLE OF EMPATHY

One scenario where we show empathy as a society is the loss of a loved one. However, I would say that in individualist societies, there is a tendency to not show emotions or feelings in public after the funeral as if the pain is expected to be over after that moment. But in reality, the pain stays for a long while. It is called grief, and it goes in circles and stages until eventually, we learn to live with a little hole in our hearts. I see people reaching out to others who are mourning, bringing food, sending cards, and truly showing up to let the person know they are there for them in this very difficult moment.

Losing someone hurts us so deeply and for such a long time. In cases like this, we demonstrate empathy. We have all been there (or will be there), and we can relate to the feeling of despair or emptiness. It is one of the most devastating emotions we feel as human beings.

What we can do is extrapolate the ability of relating to the pain another person feels and apply it to other scenarios. With time, we develop a more refined skill to relate to others who face a situation that for us is no big deal but for them is a really big deal.

We each go through life acquiring different skills. We have different personalities; we have a set of strengths and a set of areas we are constantly working on (some call it flaws, some call it our shadow side). If I were to take on a project at work, it is not a big deal for me. But imagine the person working with me has never done a project before. Practicing empathy allows me to understand how it feels to dive into an endeavor for which I have no expertise. What I relate to is not the actual scenario or situation at hand, it is the *feeling* and *emotion* the person is going through. I have been there. I understand the similarities with my own life experiences.

FIFTH EXAMPLE OF EMPATHY

Here is an example of what *not* to do from a time in my life I had yet to acquire this skill. I was teaching a class of thirty adult students. We were going through some phonetic repetition together. There was one student who was unable to get the sound correctly. As a nonempathic teacher, I proceeded to reinforce the repetition with this student while thinking in my mind, *I must not be articulating it clearly enough*. But the student burst out crying and I was dumbfounded.

How did I just make her cry? At that moment, another student raised his hand and communicated to the class that this student had just lost a loved one that day. If I had had this empathy skill back then, I would have sensed the student was not into the lesson that day, something must have happened, and I would not have assumed I needed to reinforce repetition. It was a very clear example of how we can hurt others when we don't develop the skill of empathy to communicate from the heart.

This is what empathy is about, understanding one another. **Knowing we all are different and yet the same, simultaneously**. Not expecting others to share our perspective but having the ability to relate because under different circumstances, we have faced the same emotion. That is empathy.

Empathy is love. It is telling another, I see you; I understand you, and I can feel it too.

Feeling love in our hearts is one of the most essential aspects of happiness.

What a beautiful life we can have if we are able to understand and relate with others from the heart. It does not mean we will like everybody or that we condone heinous actions because we understand their emotions. Empathy does not mean agreement. In many situations, empathy may seem impossible when we are trying to understand people who behave in unconceivable ways due to mental illness or mental disorders. We cannot condone crimes, cruelty, abuse, or neglect. But what we can try to do is empathize with how hard it must be for anyone to live in a world without a healthy brain. They are not able to think clearly and to have awareness of their own actions; devastating consequences of their actions is the outcome. At the very least, we can try to have empathy. I am personally working on this one considering how mental illness is rampant in our society. Chances are we all know of someone who suffers from it. This is one opportunity to practice empathy with a situation that is foreign to us.

I stayed home for a month when I had the bike accident. The doctor did not want me to drive. I felt confined to my home, and I felt for a moment that this is just a fraction of the feeling prisoners must experience when their freedom is taken away and they are confined to a small space day in and day out for months and years on end. I felt empathy for them in that moment. If I was feeling restless in my own home, I cannot imagine how much harder it is for another human being—or animal for that matter—to have their freedom taken away.

Imagine always being in the same place. I felt empathy for the animals in the zoo confined to small spaces and some of them in cages where they will remain all their lives, and all this for human entertainment. I felt empathy for them too because for that month, I could actually relate. The difference for me is that it was temporary. For many, it isn't.

Sometimes, I see a situation so devastating I simply cannot imagine the pain the person is going through. Consider the war against Ukraine or the war in Syria. I have not lived through a situation remotely similar to either, so to empathize with those who do, I imagine how I might feel if I went to school or work and came back to my house having been destroyed, and I am left with no place to live. How would I feel? I imagine what my life would be if I could not feel safe any minute of the day because I could be killed—or worse, tortured—at any moment. I then have at least a minuscule idea of the emotions people in the war might feel, and I feel their pain, their despair, their hopelessness. I can feel in my heart a deep pain as if it were mine.

For one moment when I imagined being in their shoes, I could feel the emotion to a much lesser degree, but I felt it nevertheless. Empathy can resensitize our hearts, so we rehumanize ourselves and start doing something for others who are in pain. It may not be political action, maybe it's monetary or activism or engagement with the cause, or perhaps it could be education for those who are not aware. It may be in the form of food or rescuing animals and helping them to have a better life, or so many other things. But none of those things would have been possible if we had not been able to empathize with those who are going through a difficult time.

Empathy moves us to action.

Empathy opens us up to feel.

Empathy reminds us that under the skin colors, heights, clothes, education, age, culture, skills, and looks, in the end we are all one. When one suffers, we all suffer. When one is happy, we are all happy. It is **the law of one.**

When we practice empathy every day, we feel connected, and we help others feel connected. It is the feeling of being seen and being heard and being acknowledged. In the end, as a human species, this is what we all need: to feel we are part of the whole—a very crucial component of happiness. When we help others feel understood, our hearts expand. We feel the light inside of us become a little brighter. It is truly a win-win situation. It takes a bit of effort, but it leads us to a more fulfilling life experience.

Imagine how much easier our interactions with others can become when we can communicate with them not just from our point of view but also from theirs. Just imagine for a moment how many arguments might be prevented, how many misunderstandings may be avoided, and how much less explaining anyone needs to do. It would be so wonderful if we all use this amazing skill of emotional intelligence. We could listen *and* speak from our hearts.

PRACTICE

What if for the next thirty days we dedicate one hour of our day to develop empathy?

For thirty days, I invite us all to intentionally identify what feelings or emotions the person we interact with is going through and allow ourselves to imagine for a moment how similar we felt in a situation of our past. It may be like something we have been through, or it may not. We can make a really good use of our imagination. How about we place ourselves in a moment when we were going through the motions in a similar way. There is no need to share our experience with the person going through a similar ordeal. The goal is to acknowledge the emotions not to compare stories. By the same token, it is not a competition either to identify who had it worst.

The goal of the practice is to develop the skill of sensing emotions in others which can help us immensely in putting ourselves in their shoes.

When we are capable of putting ourselves in their shoes, our lives will drastically change for the better. I invite us all to practice and see for ourselves.

STEP 8: BE A KID AGAIN

"If we do not have the heart of a kid, we will not enter the gates of Heaven."

—Ascended Master, Jeshua
(also known as Jesus)

I remember hearing this in church when I was a kid, and I was 100 percent in agreement with that statement. Not because I thought as a kid that only kids were worthy of going to heaven, but because only those who are not corrupted by the world and remain innocent in their hearts keep that divine essence pure and are able to connect with the realm of complete unconditional love that some people call heaven.

Let's just say heaven and hell are not actual places. They are states of being. We have talked extensively about shifting perspectives. I believe Earth can be both heaven and hell depending on how we look at life. It is that simple for me. Shifting from one to the other can happen based on circumstances but the choice of what to focus on is always ours. It is important to note that reaching a state of bliss requires purity of heart and purity of heart is present in the kids who have not been jaded by the ways of the world.

The country where my grandma raised me was big on soap operas. I remember how everybody's religion was the act of being glued to the TV after dinner watching these shows every day as if the characters were people they personally knew. They were fully invested in the characters' happiness. I distinctly remember as a kid, I heard the main character of the show tell his beloved: "Life made me this way" (as in bitter and hopeless). In that moment, the little kid in me said with a tone of absolute resolution, "I will *never* let life change me."

This has been my personal mantra. I have rebounded from trauma to find myself laughing and joyful again, just like I was before the event, and just like I was when I was a kid. I took this on as my mission in life. No matter the circumstances, I want to keep being me, and I won't let anything in life make me anything other than who I am. That kid still lives in my heart every day. I am happy, and it is the result of my intentionality, not the lack of challenges.

Let's define what kid I am talking about.

It is not the kid who knows no manners or decorum. It's not the kid who is selfish, impatient, or a bully. It's not the one who is cruel to animals or who laughs at others. No. That is not what being a kid is about. Those are behaviors of kids who are not loved for who they are and act out their hurt feelings in their distorted way of asking for love.

I am talking about the kid who discovers the world through innocent perception.

The kid who:

- Plays with all the kids regardless of how they look, where they come from, or what house they live in
- Knows no bounds of time or space and lives only in the present moment
- Centers her existence around the pursuit of joy
- Laughs without care and talks with excitement at the discovery of new things which all seem amazing and incredible
- Is mesmerized by the tiniest things like the sight of a butterfly flapping its wings

- ❖ Awakens every day with enthusiasm to experience new things in the world
- ❖ Dreams, daydreams, and lets his imagination run wild
- ❖ Loves without conditions and is immensely generous with hugs and kisses
- ❖ Gives love with no end
- ❖ Smiles because that is his heart smiling at the world and at others
- ❖ Does not know what judgment is because she sees others through her own eyes
- ❖ Loves all of nature: the plants, the trees, the soil, the pebbles. All of it is fascinating beyond words
- ❖ Is always ready to play, to have fun
- ❖ Does not want to go to sleep and miss out on the discovery of more extraordinary experiences and adventures
- ❖ Can spend hours asking questions about everything and anything because she cannot satisfy her thirst for knowledge
- ❖ Would fall sound asleep in our arms fully trusting us and knowing she is safe and cared for
- ❖ Loves all animals for the extraordinary masterpieces of creation they are
- ❖ Lives each day without thinking of the past or the future. Only now matters
- ❖ Knows friendships are her most amazing treasure
- ❖ Runs, skips, and dances in public without any care just because her little body wants to physically move all that excitement and energy of being in the world
- ❖ Feels free
- ❖ Does not give up

THAT KID!

What if we went through life embodying the mindset of a kid? What if we didn't allow life to make us bitter like that soap opera character said? What if we have the wisdom to navigate life with the maturity of an adult but the innocence of a child's heart? Who says it has to be one or the other? The secret is to have both at all times! It is possible, it is doable, and so worth it!

What if we live life to the fullest instead of just surviving day after day?

What if we relearn to thrive like kids do before society changes them?

What if we make the conscious choice to rediscover the world all over again through the eyes of our inner child who lives in our hearts?

It cannot be that hard! After all, we were there when we were kids. Certainly, we have memories of those moments that made us the happiest. How about we recreate them in an adult setting?

Seeing the world through the innocent perception of a kid's heart is the most exquisite experience one can have in life. Everything is magical. Everything is extraordinary. Everything is a wondrous discovery.

Those who have reached the status of grandparents can relate. Living a third childhood through the eyes of their grandkids is a very similar experience. Everything seems infinitely magical.

Every day is an opportunity for magical outcomes and infinite possibilities. Every day is a new beginning, a new discovery, a new adventure. Let's nurture the inner-child heart we each have.

The colors of the sky are vivid and a true piece of art we cannot get enough of. We do not take that sunrise or sunset for granted because we will see it the next day. No, we stop, we admire, we feel marveled by its beauty. We are not dismissing it because we know it rises and sets every day. Stopping to be in awe is what our inner child wants to do. Let's allow our inner child to guide us so we can start integrating this innocent perception into our daily lives and see its magic again.

Let's rediscover the world again through the eyes of our inner child.

Let's close our eyes, turn off all our devices, and be fully present at this moment.

Let's imagine ourselves as a kid, the one I described earlier. What does that feel like?

Do we remember the games we used to play when we were young? What were we most excited about when we got out of bed? Was there something we looked forward to? Perhaps it was not anything in particular.

Let's bring back the mindset of being fully present in the moment and leave the worries and cares aside.

Let's feel the love of others in our hearts and feel the burst of joy again for receiving such a wondrous gift.

I believe this is how kids see with their hearts. Adults use words as a formal linguistic exchange of communication. But communication is also happening at a nonverbal level. There are feelings behind those kind words that are filled with unconditional love frequency which children can easily sense. That is part of the mindset of seeing the world with innocent perception.

This is what can bring us happiness again.

Let's practice releasing expectations, being in the present moment, feeling the love of others, and sharing our joy freely with others. These are all things we can start with to connect with our inner child and tap into childlike joy again.

PRACTICE

For the next thirty days, I invite us all to remember the happiest moments of our childhood and recreate those memories in the setting of an adult. If our happiest memories were playing with friends, then let's get together with friends and play a board game; let's go play a sport together.

If our happiest memory was baking pies with our grandma, then go ahead and bake pies with the person closest to us and then donate the pies to a charity for example. Or eat them together at a family gathering. The important thing is to recreate those moments of joy, of connecting with a person through the action of baking.

We can consider journaling at the end of the thirty days. How has this reconnection to the dormant desires of our inner child changed our outlook about our life and the world around us?

Fun fact: I have a bumper sticker that actually says *Practice Random Acts of Kindness and Senseless Acts of Beauty*, and one day someone in a parking lot dropped a note on my windshield saying *thank you for that beautiful sticker*. Imagine how much good we can spread in the world by just practicing being a kid at heart these thirty days!

STEP 9: LETTING GO OF EXPECTATIONS

"Having expectations sabotages happiness!"

—Mother Mary

Nothing can make us more miserable than having expectations. It traps us into a fake notion of control and when life happens, as it usually does, we make ourselves miserable. It is our own expectations' doing. It all happened in our minds. Had we gone into a situation with an open mind and allowed the best outcome to unfold itself, and not just that single, specific outcome we had in mind, then life would feel more loving, more forgiving.

Expectations are ubiquitous in our society and therefore in our lives. They have been ingrained in our minds by everything and everyone around us.

Unlearning this damaging practice is an absolute must if we are to create happiness.

EXAMPLES OF DAMAGING BEHAVIORS CAUSED BY HAVING RIGID EXPECTATIONS

Example One: Thinking *I turned thirty, and I am not married. I need to find a partner ASAP.*

Age milestones seem to be triggers in society. If specific events have not happened by age X, a person feels they are lagging behind. That is an illogical expectation. Have we ever considered that not every person on this planet marches at the beat of the same drum? Each person has their own timing based on the experience in life they are meant to have.

Example Two: Believing *I need to have (fill in the blanks) in order to be happy.*

Putting happiness on hold until all material things are successfully acquired is a self-imposed expectation. Where did this expectation come from? Is it true?

Example Three: Thinking *I have to have that position at work, or I will be a failure.*

If anyone else gets the promotion I am going for, then I will be miserable and resentful and will make that person miserable too. I tie my value directly to the position I did not get at work.

If I can't have that new shiny toy then I must not be valuable enough in the eyes of others.

All these are self-imposed expectations that cause unhappiness. Where does this come from? How can we detach our value from these unrealistic expectations?

Example Four: Perpetuating this: *My kids need to always have good grades, or they are not good students.*

I am a failure as a parent if my kids have average and not the best grades.

That expectation is also self-imposed. Each kid has a different way of learning. Education systems are not adapted to all students' ways of learning. Therefore, grades are not a true indication of their intelligence and the effort they put into learning. After being a teacher myself, this is my view on this matter.

Example Five: Believing *I need to control my anxiety to be happy.*

This means, every time we struggle with anxiety, we will beat ourselves down because we do not live up to our own unrealistic expectations of living anxiety-free. That is self-inflicted pain.

Where did we get the expectation that anxiety is a blocker to happiness? Is it possible to manage it guilt-free and still be happy?

Example Six: Thinking *That trip I am taking next month has to be exactly the way I planned it and exactly the way I expect or else.*

This will set us up for inevitable disappointment because what are the chances that absolutely everything happens according to plan? Truly. That is not how life works. Can we instead adopt an open-mind mindset and go with the flow in the moment?

Example Seven: Expecting. *When I get up in the morning, turn on the TV, and notice things are the same as yesterday, I'm disappointed.*

I feel depressed, hopeless because I expected things to be better and they are not.

Chances are the bad news will continue. Will we put our happiness on hold until bad news goes away? Is that realistic?

Based on my experience, it is possible to unlearn the habit of living with expectations. It is called going with the flow or having an open mind, and it is incredibly liberating. It means, changing the thinking to *I did not get that promotion; great, it was not the best next career move for me. I will focus on my next one that will be a better fit.* When taking the trip and unexpected things happened, saying *Great, that is part of the adventure and gives me the opportunity to practice letting go. I will be surprised with new and better things I had no idea I would be able to do. My anxiety, well, it is there to remind me to be kinder to myself so when it shows up, I thank it for serving that purpose.*

Every single situation can be met with an open mind, with a desire to rise above life situations with grace and the spirit of curiosity and adventure. When expectations are not there, whatever comes is met with openness. This is truly a much better way to go through life than constantly feeling disappointed.

As in the story of the rancher and his son with a broken leg, situations at hand are neutral. They are not good or bad. It is our labeling and consequent expectation of a situation that creates unhappiness. How do expectations serve us? If they don't serve us, how can we remove them from our habits?

What if instead of expecting a specific outcome, we focus our efforts, give our best, and trust that whatever happens is there for our highest good? It will either fulfill a desire, it will culminate in an accomplishment based on consistent effort, or it is there as a lesson to learn a new way of thinking in life, a new perspective that will serve us well later.

It is so much easier said than done.

We are trained to expect a specific outcome as opposed to preparing to produce a positive one. Since we were kids, we have been taught what to expect, rather than keeping an open mind. The moment we expect a particular outcome, we narrow the potentiality of infinite possibilities to just a few because authority figures told us what to expect rather than going with the flow of the moment. Living with expectations rather than in the flow are two very different life experiences. One is restrictive and the other one is liberating. It is necessary to understand we have choices about how we approach life in order to pick the one that brings us the most joy.

We do not control anyone or anything. Expectations will be missed many times over; we will be disappointed. Life is full of surprises and those are there for a reason. It requires trusting the best possible outcome will unfold, without us knowing what that is.

Instead of expecting, we can shift our perspective to a behavior that serves us much better.

I married at twenty-five. I imagined I would have a long life with my husband and raise our daughter and enjoy life together. That was an expectation.

When he got sick, when the marriage crumbled, when the divorce happened, all my expectations were shattered into a million pieces. I felt unhappy as a result.

Years later, I look back and realize how this event catapulted me into learning about myself, and it showed me that I had far more strength in me than I had ever imagined. I feel very happy on my own and life is very fulfilling when I do all my heart desires without compromises.

If I had accepted the divorce, trusting that what would happen next would be better than the past, I would have saved myself from a lot of heartache. Instead, I fervently clung to those expectations of a happy life together that was over, and I made myself unhappy for a while.

I am grateful for this lesson. I learned to detach from the expectation and started practicing having an open mind.

There are many ways to reach a positive outcome in life. With an open mind, we can allow life to show us the path of least resistance and arrive at a better place with less effort. Therefore, we can enjoy the journey more. An example of a path of least resistance is detachment. Buddhahood is the state of detaching from the source of suffering. In this case, we can apply this to expectations. We can detach ourselves from a specific outcome, so we do not suffer when that outcome does not take place.

The Four Noble Truths in Buddhism talk about this in detail. To reach a state of bliss, we need to learn to let go, to detach. We certainly *can* do it, but it requires practice.

How can we practice letting go?

We can begin by accepting that there are other outcomes we may have never considered which may also bring us happiness.

Let me go back to my divorce example because I believe this is a common source of suffering for many.

If I had attached myself to the idea that I was *only* going to be happy with one person in life, I would never have met the wonderful people I have had in my life after my divorce. If I had spent my entire life regretting a marriage that had to come to an end, I would not have been able to keep my heart open to allow other people to walk in and bring me joy. If I had decided my ex-husband was the only person I was meant to be happy with, I would have closed the door to happiness I received from others. In other words, I went through with the divorce knowing that a chapter of my life had ended but a new chapter was about to begin. Acceptance leads to detachment.

If I had attached myself to the idea that only marriage makes me whole, I would have never enjoyed the sense of fulfillment I have as a single person.

Instead, allowing things to be and trusting that good always follows allows space for detachment to occur. It is a state of surrender. Acceptance. We may not necessarily like it at the moment, but we can start by accepting it rather than resisting it. Stopping the resistance to what is, in fact, is one of the best skills to have in life. I covered this when I shared my own personal practice.

Imagine how much suffering we can save ourselves from if we skipped the step of resisting and went directly into accepting? We would have a far less heavy heart. The intensity of the suffering would be far less. We would be able to move on at an accelerated rate.

Fast forward to today. I am, in fact, coming out of a partnership and the pain was significantly less than my divorce. The difference was that I had learned to accept and detach myself from expectations that it had to be one way or the other. It just was. It was not a walk in the park. However, the level of pain was reduced by not resisting the reality in front of me.

If we would like to become skillful in the art of detachment, I highly encourage us all to join a Buddhist meditation group like the Path to Sincerity (pathofsincerity.com) to be in a community of people who are all looking at retraining their minds to reach a state of not just nonsuffering but enlightenment too.

PRACTICE

For the next thirty days, let's start each one by releasing expectations. Just in the morning. It is already quite the task. If we catch ourselves expecting instead of being open, let's bring our mind back to the reason we are practicing this, which is to end our suffering and attain happiness.

I am going to say up front, it is not the easiest thing to do. Not because it is hard. But because we tend to have expectations at the subconscious level, so we are not even aware we have them.

However, we covered building presence and awareness in the early steps towards happiness, so this should be less difficult if we've been practicing presence. If we do struggle, however, I recommend adding another thirty days of presence practice and then try detaching from expectations again for a more fulfilling result.

As I said earlier, most of the work to be happy is in the unlearning of things rather than learning new ones. It requires an effort that is quite different from what we have done all our lives. We are all familiar with learning. We are far less familiar with *unlearning*. This is why, this particular practice will present its difficulties. We just need to keep practicing presence to develop the ability to catch ourselves when those expectations start creeping up.

Isn't it great that the key to happiness is within us already? That all we need to do is to unlearn what no longer serves us?

Isn't it wonderful to know we already have a source of happiness in our hearts, and we just need to reconnect with it because we completely forgot it has been there all along?

That is the beauty of this manual; it is a rediscovery rather than a new learning. We are already happy; we just need to stop sabotaging our own happiness on a daily basis.

STEP 10: OUR ONLY JOB IN LIFE IS TO BE HAPPY

We covered earlier the role we play in holding the frequency of unconditional love which allows those around us to receive this beautiful energy when they are in our presence. This is a big responsibility indeed. We have the power to bring others down or to uplift them. It is all about how we are managing our own energy every moment of the day. It is indeed a job.

I would like to emphasize for those of us who want to transmit healing energy to others, it starts with being in a state of joy, or gratitude, or peace. It is impossible to transmit love if we do not cultivate it first

PART 6: LEADING A HEART-CENTERED LIFE

in ourselves. It is like offering our vegetables from a garden to friends and family without ever planting the seeds for the vegetables to grow.

The same happens when we want to develop an animal energy healing practice for the well-being of our animal companions but we ourselves are not cultivating this happiness in our hearts. We then transmit the other emotions we are carrying, and chances are, they will be in detriment to their well-being. That is the opposite of what we want to accomplish. Perhaps now it is starting to make sense why our happiness is so crucial in the practice of unconditional love.

However, let's remember to give ourselves grace. There are times in life that we endure pain. It is inevitable regardless of how skilled we are in practicing presence. It is part of our life journey. It is a tapestry of experiences.

Spikey and Luna suffered with me during my most recent period of grief. I was sad, so they were sad. Luna would not move much, she kept to herself in her terrarium. She barely lifted her head. I really thought she was sick and I needed to have her checked. However, I could sense that she was experiencing sadness just like me. Spikey, on the other hand, refused to sit by me. He stared at me from the other couch across the living area. He also stopped sleeping in my bed. My sadness was so intense, he was unable to bear it. He had to keep a physical distance from me. When I walked Spikey in the neighborhood, I remember noticing how dogs started barking when we passed by. This was very unusual. I never noticed dogs barking at Spikey and me before. Then, I asked myself, *What does this series of unusual events mean?* I realized, all the animals around me were feeling my sadness and they did not like it.

My energy is very intense, and I amplify it in the space I am in. I knew I had the responsibility to manage my emotions so my energy field would not negatively impact the energy field of those animals (and humans) around me. It is inner work. It requires diligence. It is a daily effort that feels much harder when life circumstances change. Once I overcame my sadness, Luna perked up, Spikey was back by my side again, and the neighborhood dogs stopped barking. These animals were my teachers. They mirrored my emotions so I could see more clearly how I was feeling inside of me. I owed it to myself and to them to do the work and be in charge of my energy.

This is just one example of what unhappiness does all around us. Perhaps now we can understand the ripple effect our energy fields have on the rest of the world.

Think about what happens when we are happy. Externally it may show as being serene and relaxed. Perhaps it shows as being patient and tolerant. Or sometimes it may show as being more forgiving and empathetic.

We go to work, and we are able to be more patient with the situations that need to be resolved as opposed to snapping and later feeling awkward with our coworkers for losing our cool.

We see our loved ones and we can be present with them with a content and peaceful heart. They are listening to us with love, and we listen to them with love. Happiness does that. Being absent and simmering on the negative happenings of the day doesn't.

When we are happy, life seems colorful. Every little thing that goes well in our day is a cherry on top to how we already feel inside. When we are happy, we have positive behaviors like wanting to help others, volunteering, assisting people with something they need; we take the time to be more tolerant with someone who is frazzled. We feel creative, and we engage in artistic or engineering projects to channel all this wonderful positivity into creating something new. Happiness brings about our creative flow that then generates more happiness in us. As children, we loved to color, to make things, build things. Creativity is ingrained in our DNA. Allowing our creativity to flow freely *is* happiness. There is a diverse number of therapies that involve creativity to bring patients back to their homeostasis, to their inner joy state.

When we are happy, life feels lighter, issues seem easier to resolve, our minds feel clearer, and ideas flow without any blocks. **Happiness is being in the flow of life**.

When we are happy, we are at peace with ourselves. When we are at peace, we can exude peace for others to feel it too. We can then shift someone's mood with our happy hearts without saying a word. Just our presence alone is sufficient. We are all connected, and we all feel and sense each other's happiness (or lack of).

Let me ask this question: Is it possible perhaps that when we are deep in thought about all the things we consider to be negative in our life we perceive others as being short with us? Maybe rude? Perhaps dismissive? Have we noticed when we are in a more peaceful state, when we are feeling happy inside, others around us tend to greet us with a smile or interact in a more positive way? Have we noticed a correlation? If we haven't, I invite us all to check in with our inner thoughts and emotions based on how others around us respond to our presence. I guarantee that we will be able to see it. Energy does not lie.

For this reason, working on happiness truly is the purpose of our lives. Without happiness, what we spread in the world is nothing but frustration, anger, resentment, dissatisfaction, un-fulfillment, un-worthiness, failure, sadness, and the list goes on. It begs the question: the ramifications of our unhappiness, is this truly the legacy we want to leave in the world?

Harnessing happiness from within is the very core of the purpose of our existence. Happiness is what we need to attain for a pleasant journey in our life and in the lives of all around us.

How exactly can we start harnessing more happiness in our lives?

It is not what we can do for ourselves. The question is, what can we do for others? This is how we can harness happiness. Here is a recent example of how happiness changes the world around us. Last month, I woke up on Saturday morning and did my hour-long meditation, which left me in a state of profound serenity. I felt whole and in a state of contentment as I got myself ready to visit the farmers' market. I love visiting that place and being surrounded by all the wonderful people who do good things for the planet and for our health. I feel so happy walking into the market every Saturday. One of the things I love is the fact that there is no plastic. I take my baskets for produce and my growlers for my kombucha and it makes me feel so good that at least for this one day, I produce far less waste.

One day I decided to check out a pastry stand displaying decadent delights I usually pass by. For some reason I chose to go there even though I really was not craving anything in particular. There was a couple in front of me who was talking to the owner about their family. Then behind the couple was an older lady who looked a little tired or maybe a little absent but was very patiently waiting for her turn. I had still not decided what I wanted or if I even wanted anything at all.

I started to chat with the lady ahead of me and asked her what her favorite item was. She very happily engaged in the conversation with me and shared that the bread was the best. She smiled. Just talking about it made her happy. May I mention that she was a woman of color? I know I can't eliminate racism on my own. That I know. But what if I can show extra kindness to someone who I am sure has had to deal with a lot of injustice in their life? I paid for her bread. Both the owner of the pastry stand and the nice lady were speechless. I said it was my pleasure and I wished them a great day. I am sure the nice lady did not expect this when she came to the farmers' market that day. It just happened! I did not wake up knowing this is what I was going to do, I went with the flow of the moment and as a result, ended up making someone a little happier.

This is why being happy is our life purpose. Happiness has a ripple effect on others. We can brighten up someone's day with a very simple but kind gesture. It is the little things like this we do every day that add up, and before we know it, we are in fact changing the world around us.

PRACTICE

For the next thirty days, I encourage us all to dedicate one hour of our day exclusively to cultivating happiness. Each day, we can pick a different focus. For example, one day it could be the focus of leaving worries and cares aside and giving ourselves full permission to just do the activity that makes us happiest. If that means taking a nap, let's take a nap; if it means turning off everything and just sitting with our feet up and looking through the window, then let's do it. If it is baking chocolate chip cookies because they remind us of baking with our granny, then by all means, let's do that too. All that is needed is to be 100 percent present and fully savor every minute of the hour as if that is the first time we ever got to do this.

Then let's give ourselves permission to feel the pleasure of indulging in what we want to do without thinking about anyone else or anything else. Just us! This is our hour to make ourselves happy by listening to what our hearts say. We can consider adding this to our calendar and honor the time in the same way we would honor a doctor's appointment. We can take our time for happiness seriously!

Then we can journal after these thirty days. How are we starting to feel? Is there a sense of joy, of lightness in our day? Are we feeling like resting from carrying the weight of the world on our shoulders during that one hour? How has our overall happiness level changed?

Bonus: Check out the Pay It Forward website for ideas on how to pay it forward in the world too! Givingeveryday.org posts acts of kindness to spread the word and ignite more kindness.

STEP II: THE ART OF GOING WITHIN

We cannot talk about happiness without talking about enlightenment and awakening. These go hand in hand. When we achieve happiness, we are in fact awakening to the divine blueprint in us. That divine light we call Qi, Chi, Prana, Holy Spirit. There are many words for it depending on the belief system and culture. In the end, it is the core of our existence. It is the life force that makes our heart pump until we exhale our last breath. It is the energy that activates the inhalation/exhalation process of our physical bodies. It is the life force that makes all plants and trees germinate from tiny seeds or spores. It is the force that makes cells multiply to form physical bodies and be birthed by an animal or human mother. This same force of creation is in us. It is the same in every part of creation.

By going within, we return to our divine origin. We embrace our full potential: our inner power, inner wisdom, and our self-love. It is all interconnected.

When we are in touch with our divinity, the trials of the world seem to be far less overwhelming. They don't feel like our world or life is over. They feel hard, sometimes excruciatingly hard, but not insurmountable. We are starting to transcend to a realm where the only thing that matters is *being*. It is a realm some may have referred to as bliss; a place where we are all one. We are all particles of divine consciousness. This realm knows no rules or requirements; there is no north or south, no gravity, no matter, no tangible objects, no physical forms. It is the absolute presence of the unconditional love frequency. It is a vibration, and we each play a note in the orchestra of unconditional love. We each harmonize beautifully and create this consciousness together.

PART 6: LEADING A HEART-CENTERED LIFE

By going within, we connect with this life force in its purest form of energy. In this realm, the mind has no place, only the heart is able to transcend. It is like feeling bliss, nirvana, deep loving connection, enlightenment, unconditional love, peace, joy, enthusiasm, empathy, kindness, compassion, happiness, and fulfillment, all at the same time.

When we go within and connect to our divinity, we feel complete, we feel whole. It is a feeling like nothing else in the world.

It does take effort to go within.

In addition to the steps mentioned earlier in the Self-Love Guide and how to cultivate unconditional love frequency, I also set myself on a mission to truly learn as much as possible about everything that could help me go within.

My intent with this section is to present a cornucopia of choices for going within. Let's enjoy the exploration! Most importantly, let's enjoy the process. Going within is not a destination either. It is a constant unfolding of self-discovery and self-mastery. We know we are on the right path when we find the practice that nourishes our soul. We will feel we have arrived home. We owe it to ourselves to stay with it. And practice!

After having a taste of all these, I stayed with animal energy healing as my primary pillar of enlightenment. My recommendation is to go on our own discovery journey to sample the different modalities that call our name—the ones we have an affinity for, the ones that *feel* right. We can then connect in person with the people who teach them and see how they resonate with us.

Here is my story of self-discovery, of going within.

There was a time in my life when I needed everything to be "perfect." Funny, as if perfection is even real! But there I was, obsessing over getting things done as perfectly as possible. I was one of those stressed-out people going to bed and unable to sleep as I ran over my to-do list for the next day. I consistently neglected to give myself a chance to decompress and rest. I was that mom who planned every minute of the day to make sure everything got done, never considering for a second if doing it all made me happy. I would pick up even more things to do during the weekend out of a sense of duty as opposed to giving myself the rest I actually needed. I aimed at being hyperproductive and making my child happy. I did not aim at being happy myself necessarily; that idea was not my focus. My child was my first priority, and my job was my second priority.

During these years of raising a child, there were two books that caught my attention. They were *The Power of Now* and *The New Earth* by Eckhart Tolle. I read them both and something in me shifted. I was inspired to learn more about quieting my mind and understanding detachment from the image of self in order to connect with that inner light.

At a minimum, I wanted to be able to sleep. So how exactly did I learn to quiet my mind?

First, I followed a Buddhist practice podcast to learn to meditate. I needed someone to guide me. I could not figure out how to do it on my own. That podcast was excellent. I started to play with the idea of actually relaxing my mind and not generating thoughts as I conducted activities around the house. I would practice mindful dishwashing, mindful driving, mindful everything. I realized how malleable my mind actually was. It was in fact possible to change those overactive thinking patterns and give myself a mental reprieve.

Next, I visited Buddhist temples for weekend retreats so I could be immersed in the community and learn more. Something about being together working toward the same goal—in this case, meditation—was very fulfilling for me. It gave me the boost I was not getting

PART 6: LEADING A HEART-CENTERED LIFE

from the podcasts because I was lacking the very needed sense of community. For the purpose of clarification, I do not ascribe myself to any religion. However, I mention Buddhism because in their philosophy, meditation is the foundation of the practice. I wanted to learn from those I consider experts in quieting the mind.

As I got an idea about meditation, I started reading more about spirituality. I read a few of Deepak Chopra's books and carved out time to be with myself. This was a game changer for me. It shifted another aspect in me. I realized this: It is not just OK but essential to give time to myself every day. Why is that important? Because to go within, the very first step is to honor ourselves. We need time to do that. How will we ever be able to achieve a deeper connection to our essence?

My life continued for a few years like this, practicing meditation. Reading. Learning. I felt I was in a good place but yearned for more. I knew there was more to life than just fulfilling obligations day in and day out and giving an hour to myself. I knew there had to be more meaning to life than this. I wanted to understand what role I played in all of creation. What is this awareness that observes from outside the identity of the ego? Religion did not have any of those answers for me, only conditions, rules, and an array of misinterpretations of what love actually is. Society did not have any answers for me either. Education did not provide any answers—no surprise there. It was up to me to search for myself and discover. I really wanted to understand this light inside of me, this awareness.

At that time, my uncle who was an avid Catholic asked me to connect with the angels. My first question was why? But I love my uncle; he was like a grandfather to me and my daughter and without thinking twice I started looking into angels and seeing what might resonate.

I found the Archangel Raphael channeler Kelly Kolodney back in 2011 or 2012 when she was interviewed by a podcaster I used to follow.

Something in her voice resonated. I felt she was genuinely full of love, and I decided to connect with her. Early in her journey, she was not teaching classes regularly but doing sessions over the phone or in small gatherings in person in her hometown—in a different state. So, I signed up to do a couple of sessions over the phone and connected with Archangel Raphael, the angel of healing who resides in our heart chakra.

It was a sublime experience for me. I realized I had just arrived at the place I was meant to be. This wonderful channeler then started to do classes on the phone (before visual platforms) and I took every single one of them to awaken the divine blueprint in me, to help me connect deeper with my heart, with the heart of others, and with all of creation. I took classes on how to connect with the Earth and with each of the elements and how to connect with the Ascended Masters (and most recently Kelly Kolodney is teaching light codes to connect with the frequency that is present on Earth, in other realms, and to connect with the loving galactic beings who assist us on Earth). She has a great YouTube following. Over a decade later, I still follow her teachings.

Kolodney's classes completely changed me. I was able to go within and connect with my heart, with my higher self, and with Spirit. I learned to receive direct divine wisdom to provide clarity in the different events in my life and my path, my purpose, and my understanding of my presence on Earth. Once I was able to go within at this level, the opening of the universal library of knowledge became fully available to me whenever I connected. All I needed to do was ask and the answer would be there. I learned that the gift I had developed was claircognizance which is clear knowing. This feels like having full certainty of the information received. For example, if I was offered this new position at work, I would ask, *Should I take it?* The answer was a sense of my full body feeling right: zero anxiety, zero apprehension, zero self-doubt, zero hesitation. That is claircognizance. The knowledge is clear and certain with absolutely no doubt whatsoever. That was amazing! Having that connection to my higher self makes day-to-day life easier. It does not eliminate challenges. I still go through rough times, but I know they will bend me but never break me.

My quest for enlightenment continued. I connected with a wonderful lady nearby who channels Mother Mary. I was delighted because I have been very close to the energy of Mother Mary all my life. When I was a kid, my house was right in front of the Basilica of the Lady of the Angels. I was excited to have found someone who channels her! I looked forward to conversations with Mother Mary as channeled by Barb. It was absolutely magical for me. We are now great friends, and I am so grateful for her. She is Reverend Barbara Beach, and she has a blog of Mother Mary letters where she posts channeled messages from Mother Mary every week and conducts private sessions per request. I highly recommend my friend Barb, her channeling accounts of Mother Mary are so full of unconditional love.

The conversations with Mother Mary and the lessons with Archangel Raphael continued in parallel. They both work primarily with the heart chakra. Their energy is the unconditional love frequency. They feel like arriving at nirvana. The sense of bliss is ineffable. I had at this point in my life started to have one foot in this realm and the other foot in the unconditional love realm. I started to see the world differently: no longer caught up in perfectionism. I was no longer dwelling in the past. I remained more present in the now for most of my day, each day.

To continue learning, I also enrolled in a membership with Hay House website to take as many of the online courses they have available as I could: crystals, Kabbalah, mediumship, and more on angels. I was fully dedicated to learning. I learned online for two years. However, I did not feel satisfied; I needed community. In this part of my life, I started feeling more genuinely connected with people. Small talk seemed to be a thing of the past; I was more interested in getting to know those around me: have deeper conversations, understand them better, see our similarities.

As a result of this, I attended metaphysical fairs in person, and connected with channelers, intuitives, and other practitioners. Talking face to face gave me the opportunity to have a taste for the different modalities providing routes to going within and connecting with my higher self at a deeper level. I was truly taking it all in like a kid in a candy store. I was so marveled by this metaphysical world that I had always been intrigued with but never had envisioned myself having it this accessible for exploration.

It was around this time when this friend Barb, who channels Mother Mary, asked me if I wanted to learn Reiki, to which I said, "Absolutely!" At that moment, I already had an idea what healing powers energy has. I was quite interested in learning and getting a certification. That story, as I have shared already, is what led me to being an animal energy healing practitioner. In my own words Animal Reiki is nothing but mastering the art of holding the frequency of unconditional love in the heart while connected with the higher power and transmitting it to the animals we love. As a result of this learning, I have spent years helping animals and learning from them how to love even more deeply.

Fast forward to when my daughter got sick and suffered a mental health crisis. My search for enlightenment accelerated. All I had learned to that point was not enough to stop me from going into deep darkness. I needed answers about her well-being. I needed to find the light out of the darkness. The emotions had clogged my channel to my higher self, and I was back in my mind worrying and stressing over the situation. In order to reconnect, I signed up for a shamanic retreat in Mount Shasta for a week that same summer of her crisis. I had never camped under the stars before, had no real idea what shamanism was about—no clue—but I knew I needed to find hope again. My light had dimmed, and I knew reconnecting with the Earth and with my inner light would help. The retreat would show me how.

This retreat did in fact teach me how to deeply connect to the Earth, to ground myself, to connect with the wind, the earth, the fire, and the water in nature who reside also within me. We chanted; we used a rattle to get into a meditative state. We spent time dancing around the fire in a circle, chanting songs to nature, honoring nature. The cows grazing in vast fields very far away from us would come running and line up to observe us dancing around the fire. I was fascinated that we had built a community not only with human beings but with all creatures. The loving frequency generated during those dances was pretty spectacular. My heart was starting to find inner peace again.

We honored the four directions and talked to each as if they were loving wise guides listening to us and ready to provide support and love. It was not a plant medicine retreat. There were no substances other than vegan food and fresh water from the spring. This retreat took me to a state of presence. It allowed me to get out of my incessant thoughts of worry for my daughter and reminded me how I could stay present in my body to get through those moments knowing it too would pass. It took a few months, but I knew all along I was going to make it. It was excruciatingly painful, but I made it. At this point in my spiritual journey, I had acquired a very solid foundation of grounding myself. This is a crucial skill when it comes to navigating life's challenges.

This set me off on a quest for more spiritual retreats. I had a taste for what it was like to connect to the elements; I wanted to connect to all of creation. I wanted to feel the oneness that connects us all. I wanted to fuse more deeply with my higher self and continue to receive guidance that would help me on my journey. I have always been on a quest but this time it truly accelerated. The crisis of my daughter served as a catalyst for my enlightenment. **Enlightenment is not a destination, it is a journey**. Each day I learn more and as a result, I open up more.

At a certain point, I decided to go to the South of France to experience the power of a very beautiful divine feminine energy called Mary Magdalene. A misogynist pope in the fourth century was responsible for changing the religious scripts to portray an erroneous image of her. This brutal image lasted for centuries until finally in 1969 her name was cleared by the religious supreme authority and in 2016, she got her official feast day, July 22 to join the rest of her male counterpart apostles whose images were never tarnished. The pope in the fourth century, would not tolerate a woman at such a high level of sanctity, so he removed her from the older scriptures. Mary Magdalene is an incredibly powerful energy of love, as powerful as Jeshua's energy, as it is recorded in stories of the people of the land where she lived after the crucifixion. The two together brought the light into the world.

I was very interested in learning the truth and visiting the sacred sites where she lived, and I wanted to be in a deep connection with her divine energy. So I did. I started receiving messages from her about how to hold a loving heart in what seems to be an unforgiving world. I received messages about strength and courage that remain true in my heart. When I need to remind myself of my inner strength during a dark time, I think of the words I received from her during this retreat. I felt that as women, we too have an ingrained sense in our hearts of what it is like to not be honored equally to our male counterparts. At this stage in my journey, I started feeling empowered. I felt a sense of confidence and inner knowing I had not experienced before. This retreat left me feeling a sense of deep connection to my inner light.

I also visited Egypt and connected to the ancient mysteries of ascension. I learned that ascension, another word for transcending the physical to reach the realm of pure unconditional love frequency, was the purpose of the temples and pyramids present in Egypt according to what is encoded in the walls of the pyramids.

While there, I felt for the first time my soul leaving my body and connecting with one of my spirit guides who of course happened to be Egyptian. I was with a group of spiritual seekers with the same incredible light shower of a guide, Dana Micucci, who had also led me in the Mary Magdalene retreat. Dana is also a published author of the book about Mary Magdalene, *The Third Muse*, a wonderful portrayal of the divinity of this feminine Ascended Master.

Egypt and Southern France started opening the rest of my chakras, and I began seeing more through my third eye. My clairvoyance had been activated. I had also sporadically experienced Spirit through my other senses like smell and hearing, not just my sight. But those were not happening as frequently as receiving images in my mind. Developing clairvoyance meant I could see more of the energy of a situation or an animal or a person. I remember going to yoga and seeing the entire floor sparkle, almost like the glistening quality of the sunlight reflecting on the ice crystals of the snow after a fresh snowfall. It has been magical to have my third eye activated. I see the walls in my home as undulating, vibrating energy rather than a solid mass of wood or concrete. It is like the movement of a sea of subtle energy. My most commonly used clair- remains claircognizance. However, I do frequently see images of events that happened or are going to happen.

There is always a purpose for receiving this information. I do not walk around knowing everything about everyone. That would be an invasion of privacy and quite honestly, very overwhelming. It is more of a request for information with the permission of the person or animal in question. If they are in agreement, the information will reveal itself.

As my spiritual journey continued, I learned to do a more science-based approach to connect within with a modality called HeartMath. A friend of mine who is a phenomenal shamanic practitioner teaches this method to veterans to help overcome the trauma of fighting in war. Connecting within is another way of getting out of our overactive, unforgiving minds and dropping into the loving presence of our hearts. Our hearts, not our minds, have the answers. **The heart, not the mind, gives us peace.** HeartMath uses sensors to measure the brain waves as the person focuses their attention on their hearts.

The sensor lights up green if the person wearing the sensors is in a pure state of heart coherence. It is yellow if the person is in between their heart coherence and the overactive mind. Finally, the light will turn red if their hearts are no longer in a coherent state. What is elucidating about using a sensor is getting instantaneous feedback of how our thoughts disrupt the peace. We can see by the color of the lights, how are thoughts disrupt our heart coherence or enhance it. For those of us who need tangible proof of the benefits of mindfulness, this is a great method. Traumas, emotional wounds, hurt feelings, grief, etc., all those trapped energies in the heart start healing with love and peace frequencies—HeartMath can be a great modality to release them.

I love learning, and my spiritual journey has been filled with great experiences. For this reason, when I was asked to take a business trip to India, I took a few extra days to go on my own and visit sacred sites in the northern part of the country. I captured rainbow orbs in my pictures. These orbs were the presence of Spirit, specifically Mother

Mary, letting me know she was with me. Capturing images with the lens of a camera that the naked eye cannot see, is always an exciting experience. It was not until I had time to review the photos I had taken that I realized the rainbows were there. I feel as if Spirit was stopping by to say hi and shower me with unconditional love.

At this point in my journey, I had been meditating every day. As suggested by one of the fellow students in one of Kelly Kolodney's classes, we downloaded the Insight Timer app on our phones to track time spent and consecutive days in meditation. With that competitive tactic, I was able to build a consistent practice of meditation I have kept for over a decade now. Today, if I do not start with meditation, I am off balance all day. I don't feel grounded. I don't feel myself. I cannot leave my house without meditating. It has become crucial for me.

This trip to sacred places in India left me feeling more connected than ever. I felt a deep sense of peace in the knowing that we are that I AM presence I had heard so much about and I was finally feeling deep inside of me. This trip showed me how to detach from my ego and connect with this divine presence. The energy of the sacred sites facilitates this connection.

What happens when we connect with our divine essence? I receive a flow of messages my higher self has for me. I receive words, images, or a deep and clear knowing. I feel uplifted; I visit the realm of unconditional love frequency. I detach from my ego mind, and I am pure awareness. During meditation, I close my eyes, play soft melodic solfeggio music, and I allow myself to feel grounded with the core of the Earth. This connects me to the higher power, and I feel I have arrived home. It's a state of bliss, of infinite serenity, and of pure harmony. I breathe in and I breathe out with intention, knowing each breath brings Spirit into my physical body. I exhale and I feel my aura expand to cover the perimeter of the entire room I am in, of my house even. I feel expansive and whole. My heart feels like a pulsating divine force present in the entire universe. This is what my meditations feel like. I only need to close my eyes and bliss follows. This is how I start my day.

In parallel to my learning pursuit, I also connected with a professional psychic-medium, Sharon Sananda, who teaches various psychic classes. I signed up to be in her classes as her intern for six months, but I continued learning from her classes for at least another three years. During this time, I learned about lucid dreaming, how to connect with my twin flame, how to take photographs of orbs or plasma clouds, to scry, to connect with other angels, Ascended Masters, and Spirit Guides. I learned how to help earthbound spirits cross into the light, to use the spirit box, to connect with my past lives, to channel, and to connect with those who have departed.

We also did table tipping, spoon bending, and automatic writing. She is so gifted and has amazing experiences of near death to tell the world. She recently published her book on this topic. Incredible! I learned a lot from Sharon, and she is now a dear friend of mine. We even did psychic experiments together for over two years and met every other Tuesday with other dear friends to practice connecting with Spirit by channeling and table tipping. These couple of years were phenomenal. The door had been open to experience energy in unlimited ways. I felt this was a gift and I was meant to be in service of those who need it. I do not specifically go looking for earthbound souls; however, if I do come across one, I know now how to help them cross into the light. This has been one of the unplanned benefits of my spiritual journey.

I also use oracle card decks to connect with Spirit. I bought several oracle card decks of animals, portals, Ascended Masters, angels, Mother Mary, fairies, and others. I still use them regularly to do readings for someone or for myself. I do love using cards because it is not the guidance written in the book that matters most but the messages I receive as I look into the details of the image on the card. I have realized that cards have always been spot on regarding the question or concern I have. It is not a yes/no question I am searching for. I am asking for the meaning of something that has taken place. Spirit communicates to me very clearly through cards. It is a way of deciphering the never-ending cryptic messages of life's infinite twists and turns, which I have had a pretty good share of myself.

What I learned with Sharon has been integrated in my day-to-day life. Yes, I can bend spoons; yes, I can tip tables; yes, I can channel; yes, I can do automatic writing. Yes to all. "It is not hard," she told all her students. "It requires two main things: intention and belief. Where our focus is, our energy goes and things do happen." Connection takes place. It is absolutely fascinating! During past life classes I was able to see several of my past lives in detail: where I lived, what geographic location, what time in history, what I was doing, and, in some of them, how I died. But for the most part, I connected to how happy I was in certain lives, and the things I did that fulfilled me. Understanding where my likes and dislikes originated from was a revelation. I also received readings from her explaining why certain blood relatives had strong desires to see me unhappy in this life. It is due to unresolved karmic events in previous lifetimes that carried over into this one.

Life doesn't happen by chance. Everything is meant to delight us or to teach us something. Nothing happens just because. One way of going within is to have an open heart and ask the question, **What is the lesson for me here?** The heart will answer if only we are ready to listen. These three years learning from Sharon allowed me to acquire a myriad of spiritual tools for situations at hand. I started to feel more and more in my power and with that comes the responsibility of using these tools to be of service. I very quickly understood this was not meant to be exclusively for my personal benefit.

Upon invitation from a shamanic practitioner in my circle of friends, I experienced a mushroom journey and then a San Pedro journey. This practitioner is an amazing doula healer who assists those who are transitioning in having a peaceful letting go as they die. What a gift this is to the world. How many people fear death because they do not know what it is? During these journeys, my heart opened to the Oneness of the universe even more. It was an ineffable experience; however, I will make an attempt at describing it.

The plant medicines connected me to the Oneness of all that is. It was what many call the "death of the ego." I was no longer a person with a name, I was part of the whole, and I experienced what it feels like to be water—what it feels like to be nothing and everything all at once. No shape, no form, just energy, and an overwhelming feeling of Oneness and love that brought me to tears. The love was overflowing and expansive, and it was a love I had never felt so intensely before. It was as if for this time, I was life itself. I was love itself. I was the universe itself, and I could feel the pulsating life force fueling it all. When plant medicine wears off, the mind starts to come back and along with it, the remembering of being human and having a physical experience on Earth. It was sad in a way to come back to this type of reduced existence after experiencing the expansiveness of infinite Oneness. The documentary called *Fantastic Fungi* is a wonderful narration of how amazing it is to use plant medicine to connect to the divine blueprint, the I AM presence, the sublime unconditional love frequency for which there are no words. I highly recommend this documentary. It may shift the perspective on the expansive and limitless miracle of life.

I learned from working with plant medicine to hold the frequency even if I am not taking plant medicine anymore. The frequency has been awakened in my heart, so I nourish it and cherish it and keep it vibrant and alive. This is the same unconditional love frequency I transmit to animals during my energy healing sessions. My practice started with Reiki, but I have incorporated so much of what I have learned to this point that it would be inaccurate to call my practice Reiki. I call it energy healing instead. Because I work primarily with animals, it is more appropriate to say *animal energy healing practice*. However, I truly work with everyone.

After experiencing plant medicine, my perspective of life shifted. I was able to quiet my mind. My heart was in charge the vast majority of my day, and this continues to be the case today. Experiencing life through the heart, not the mind is a richer experience. It does not mean challenges do not come up; it means I can see into the deeper meaning of it. This gives me more peace. I know I will feel pain in situations, but now I know the purpose of it.

Another practice I incorporated in my spiritual path of awakening is sacred geometry. I knew nothing about sacred geometry, but my curious and open mind enrolled me in a class at my favorite metaphysical bookstore, New Renaissance in Portland. I was in awe at what happened in the class. The two hours of drawing the seed of life and flower of life for the first time in my life disconnected me from my body and took me to that space of Oneness again—that sublime feeling of connection with All That Is. This mathematical representation of divine light had activated the divine blueprint in me. At the end of the class, the instructor, a wonderful lady called Nadi, asked all the students in the class to write our name on a piece of paper if we wanted to be added to her newsletter. She was a former mental health practitioner who was fully immersed in her spiritual path, and she was just starting to teach classes. I could not write my name for a few minutes. My mind said, *Oh wait a second; what am I called in this existence?*

Never in my life had I been so transfixed on anything that I had forgotten I had a name. This was the clearest sign of how extraordinarily powerful sacred geometry is. I continued learning with Nadi for several years until her recent passing. I have lots and lots of gorgeous artwork in my beautiful home thanks to her patient instruction and loving presence. Temporary Temples website from the UK teaches sacred geometry too and Nadi learned from them. I am fortunate to continue my learning under the instruction of Temporary Temples. Thanks to this practice I feel more attuned to the building blocks of creation. Sacred geometry is how the universe came to be in physical form. The platonic solids are present in everything and everyone. Absolutely fascinating!

This brings me to the COVID era. During this time, the focus of my spiritual learning went toward connecting with the Galactics, beings from other planets, and with the Dragon energy.

During 2020, I dedicated my free time to taking classes with Galactic Ashley who is deeply connected to the higher technology of advanced beings of light on other planets. There is so much to learn. Our very limited human brains do not have the capacity to truly comprehend the connection we have with the stars. **We are made of stardust.** We originated from the stars. Yet, we have so much hesitation in remembering the truth of life outside of Earth.

For a complete year, I learned additional methods of going within to connect more and more. Each time, more magical things happened in my life. It is empowering to co-create our reality when we are aligned with our divine essence. It was around this time I met my partner and had a very beautiful relationship for the following three-and-a-half years. How fun it was to have a kindred spirit by my side for that period of time.

I did other spiritual retreats in England, Ireland, and Scotland. I met Glenn and Cameron from Journeys with Soul (www.journeyswithsoul.com), who are both incredibly gifted beings of light. I embarked on the discovery of my inner light again, this time plugging my energy into the ley lines of the Earth and connecting with the power of this beautiful planet we call home. I also connected with ancient sites and in particular Newgrange in Ireland where the energy of the place was so strong it made me dizzy for a few moments. The currents of energy present on Earth intensify in places where people have gathered to honor the Earth, to be in community. We, together, have tremendous power. When we are in community, we tap into that power. We just need to remember how hard it was for many to be isolated during 2020. It affected many in a very deep way. We take the power of community for granted because we have always had it available. When we did not have it, we could finally understand what a driving force it is in our existence. These retreats in the British Isles and Ireland left me feeling more attuned to Mother Earth. Visiting the sites where the ley lines intersect is quite extraordinary. They are a network of electromagnetic forces that interact with all of us in ways I had not had the opportunity to feel before. Visiting them helped me feel more connected to Mother Earth in a completely new way.

Retreats are incredibly effective in raising my frequency and taking me to the next level of my spiritual journey. I felt the energy within as if I was going to burst with joy. It was exhilarating! Being in community, dedicating days of my life exclusively to the pursuit of my enlightenment, connecting with the geomagnetic currents of the planet, the ley lines, and the sacredness of the sites, along with the incredibly healing forces that Dana, Glenn, and Cameron are, raised my frequency exponentially.

Gong sound baths are another way to go within. I have been following Wayne Marto from Beneficial Sound for almost a decade now—since his humble beginnings—and I have learned that the power of sound frequency in the body can create a spontaneous entrainment leading to connection within. The vibration of the gong emits a high frequency energy that pushes stagnate emotional energy—the source of all ailments—out of the body. It has great healing power. Attending a gong sound bath may dislodge repressed grief, anger, or fear. By dislodging it, it can finally be cleared. Wayne is amazing. I attended a gong sound bath retreat with him recently which left me feeling like I was walking on clouds.

I hope this manual has provided ideas and tools to help all of us to connect to our divine selves as well. I hope this serves as a guideline to know where to start taking those precious baby steps to find our own path of connection.

Living a happier, more enlightened life will give us all:

- Inner wisdom to make decisions that are aligned with our highest good
- Serenity when others' emotions are explosive and ours are calm and collected
- A different perspective when all other people can see is doom and gloom
- An inextinguishable hope because we know we are supported through the darkest times
- Strength that comes from knowing the inner light in our hearts and their indescribable power
- A joy that comes from knowing we are not defined by roles, things, or anything physical
- Inner peace that comes from the connection with it all, independent of transient situations

- ❖ A pure love that is not based on reciprocity or gain. It is just the pure expression of our divine nature

Through our hearts, we have access to the ancient wisdom of our elders, protectors, guides, and higher selves because the heart is the gateway to higher realms. We cannot access this until we have a heart unburdened by the world, still and at peace. When we can learn to connect by going within, we find we can then become one with All That Is, including the hearts of others.

In order to reach a state of blissful happiness in this world, we need to just close our eyes and connect with ourselves.

Listen to your heart.

Truly listen.

Once we are connected to our hearts, happiness follows.

The clearest evidence of our connection to our divinity is joy, one of the highest frequencies in the universe. **When we have found joy, we have found ourselves.** There is no going back.

Continuing our journey without looking harshly on the learnings of our younger selves is key. Looking ahead and continuing to extract wisdom from what our challenges teach us is our divine purpose. Connecting within is not a destination, it is a journey, and the goal is to enjoy this ride and allow magic to unfold every day, through the ebb and flow of this beautiful river we call life.

I urge all of us to feel fully the joy and the heartbreak.

That is what living with an open heart is all about.

Closing our hearts up in fear of hurting is barely surviving in life. We are meant to thrive.

Let's embrace the ebbs and flows of this river.

Let's love our minds for keeping us safe, and let's live in our hearts while giving our minds time to rest.

The heart is the sage, and the mind is the apprentice.

Let's allow the inner child to be our guide so we may always find our way back into our hearts.

Let's use the acquired wisdom to not just live but thrive.

Archangel Raphael has said that **love is always the answer**. Life is beautiful when we choose to stay centered, balanced and in our hearts.

"Do the best you can until you know better.

Then when you know better, do better."

—Maya Angelou

Once we have acquired tools to elevate our frequency and have deepened our connection to our light, we are then ready to work with these beautiful creatures we call animals. In this last chapter, I have put it all together in hopes that if we all love animals the way I do, my animal energy healing technique can inspire us all to be our own version of animal energy healers in service to these wondrous beings of unconditional love. In return, they will be thrilled to share their wisdom on how to live our lives with an open heart.

PART 7
BATHE ANIMAL COMPANIONS WITH THE FREQUENCY OF LOVE

If the stories I shared earlier in the book have inspired us to learn more about how energy can be a powerful force of change in the world of animals, I would like to extend the invitation to consider learning some of the techniques I use in my animal healing practice. Not only does it improve the emotional, mental, and physical well-being of the animals, but also of their human guardians too. It is a symbiotic relationship that has no limits. We will find it to be a source of amazement! Loving frequency does indeed work in so many marvelous ways. There are no contraindications to this practice.

If we are ready to try it out, here are some of my basic techniques to use with animals to assist them in raising their frequency. The secret is to work on self first before working on the animal. After all, **we cannot give what we do not have.** I hope by now this book has provided clarity on that fundamental truth. First, it is essential to harness the unconditional love in our hearts before trying to send it to the animal.

MY ANIMAL ENERGY HEALING TECHNIQUE

We remember that animals are wise, higher frequency beings who will always know how to best utilize the unconditional love frequency we share with them. Therefore, let's make sure we keep in mind that we are being of service, but it is they who have the final say on how the energy will be utilized and for what specific outcome. All we can do is witness what will unfold after we share the unconditional love frequency with them. Good things always happen. We just need to be open to them all and allow the animal to be in charge while we provide a service, one void of expectations.

Over years of working with animals, I have integrated what I have learned through certifications, books, courses, and my own experience, and I have condensed it into these very simple steps that anyone can follow to harness the healing power that comes from a genuinely loving heart. Each technique is slightly different, and it is meant to be adjusted to what feels right for each person and for each specific situation. Everyone is also different; therefore, one technique may feel too intense while another may feel not powerful enough. It is important to practice, assess, and adjust accordingly until each of us finds the technique that fits best. We will know when this happens because it will be natural, effortless, and will fill us with an inner sense of knowing that this is the right approach.

There are three prerequisites before the session with the animal can be initiated. These preliminary steps are geared toward energy hygiene to ensure we are in the right space to be transmitters of unconditional loving energy.

Step 1: We remove all expectations of the outcome of the session. This may require a pleasant walk or a time in nature to bring ourselves to a place of acceptance with any outcome that comes from the session.

Step 2: We take a deep, cleansing breath and release all the worries, frustrations, anger, or fears absorbed during the day and bring ourselves to a state of peace and calmness. Remember the importance of practicing self-regulation. This may require utilizing techniques to regulate our nervous system. Perhaps tea, music, a run. Reset the nervous system and be in full receiving and giving mode.

Step 3: We intend to receive an energetic shower of high unconditional love frequency that washes away any residue of low frequency energies that stayed behind after completing Step 2.

After completing these preliminary steps and having a clear energetic field to work with, it is now time to prepare the space for the session to start.

Step 4: We create a space that is suitable for the energy to be transmitted to the animal. We may choose a small table where we can light a candle, or incense, and a space for any crystals we may have. Malachite is great for healing and clear quartz for amplification of the unconditional love frequency we will send. We will desire physical comfort, so let's not forget to have a cushion and perhaps instrumental music (432Hz music is a good choice). Create a setting that will have minimal to no disruptions: cell phone, TV, electronics are all off. Ensure the light shining on the space is not disruptive. Then we prepare a space conducive to peace, serenity, and comfort. We will be here for an hour or so and we will want the entire area to be inviting, relaxing, and warm. Essential oils are a wonderful way to create an ambiance that opens the heart and invites love to flow. Floral scents, woody scents, or even citrusy scents are wonderful: I personally use rose essential oil to open my heart chakra. Each of us will want what works for us.

Step 5: We drink a glass of water. We can hold it in our hands, and practice gratitude for the hydration this will bring to every cell in our bodies. Let's drink this water with the intention of purifying the body, which will be the conductor of the energy we will then send to our animal companion. Energy flows with ease when the body is well hydrated.

Step 6: We will then call in our Spirit Guides and all the beautiful beings of light that we trust in our life. This can be angels, Ascended Masters, Mother Mary, Jeshua, Galactics, Dragons, Mary Magdalene, the choice is all ours. These are just examples of the ones I call into my practice to assist me in each of my sessions. But we can call in the higher frequency beings that resonate with each of us—the ones that are true to our personal experience.

Step 7: We set the intention of what we would like this unconditional love frequency healing to bring: healing, health, balance. Say it out loud. We can each adapt our own intention that feels right for the situation at hand. For example, "I intend with this energy healing to bring better physical, emotional, mental health to this beloved animal companion. May he use this unconditional love frequency in any way he feels is needed for his well-being and if desired, to be stored for later use. I remove any expectations of the outcome of this session, and I trust that he will utilize this energy for his highest and greatest good. And so it is."

Step 8: We take three deep breaths to initiate the session. This allows the body to be in complete surrender mode and able to conduct the energy that will be received and transmitted to the beloved animal companion. Remember, the energy is not coming from us but through us. This is why the preliminary steps are crucial in clearing ourselves to be in full receiving mode for the transmission to take place effectively.

Step 9: We visualize a beam of light coming from above, passing through the crown chakra and going to the heart. This beam of light is an intense golden, white light, and it is coming in strong. We may

PART 7: BATHE ANIMAL COMPANIONS WITH THE FREQUENCY OF LOVE

feel in our bodies an energized, almost a tingling, sensation; each person is different. This light is connecting us to the unconditional love frequency of Source and the receptacle is our hearts. Visualize our hearts charged with this golden, white light. The light has a distinct quality that feels warm and loving.

Step 10: We visualize now another beam of light, a pale rose color of unconditional love frequency coming from the core of the Earth, coming up through our feet, legs, and into our hearts to merge with the energy we are receiving from above. The two unconditional love frequencies fuse into one at the heart level and form the shape of an infinity sign. We can visualize this unconditional love frequency moving in the figure-eight direction. It is not a static infinity sign but an ever flowing energy in constant motion at the heart level.

Step 11: Now let's visualize, or imagine, a surge of high frequency energy circulating in our hearts. This will be projected towards our beloved animal companion, and she will receive it with an open heart. It is as if the energy is bathing the animal in this high frequency now reaching every single cell in her body. The animal looks luminous. It is almost blinding how intense the energy is.

Step 12: We then focus all our attention on how much we love this animal. Focus on the love the animal has for us also. We hold that feeling, that emotion in our hearts. We hold it and avoid any thoughts that may try to come into our minds. If thoughts come, we dismiss them and get back to holding the love. Feel our hearts expanding, growing, being amplified.

The more we focus on the love we have for this animal, the more our hearts expand, and the more intense the unconditional love frequency becomes. Hold that feeling of love. No thoughts, no expectations, simply hold the love frequency that goes from our hearts to theirs. **This is the core of the session.**

Step 13: We visualize this love penetrating every single organ, bone, muscle, vein, artery in our animal's body. The light is not just projected on her, it is now inside of her. It is in every chakra, in all organs, and it is circulating in every artery. The animal is shining from inside out. Hold the feeling of love for the animal—love for every part of her body, every part of her being, all the way to her cellular structure.

Step 14: We stay in this space for as long as we can. We hold and work our way to thirty or forty-five minutes. The energy may feel intense. The animal may choose to walk away as it may be enough for one session. In any case, we always allow what unfolds. What unfolds in this moment of high frequency is exactly what is needed.

Step 15: We visualize the beam of light starting to dim and retract. Our hearts start coming back to their normal size. The beam from the core of the Earth returns to the core of the Earth. The beam from above retracts and returns to the sun. Our hearts are now their normal size; the unconditional love frequency is no longer being projected to the animal.

Step 16: We visualize now that with our hand, we are making a swift motion as if cutting any energetic cords that remain between our animal companion and us. This is not going to cut the bond we mutually have; this is only going to complete the unconditional love frequency transmission, so our energy is not drained by keeping the session open indefinitely. That would be the equivalent of leaving our house lights on all day and night.

Step 17: We thank our animal companion for accepting this offering of love that we intended as a sign of our love for their highest and greatest good. We thank the animal for giving us the opportunity to be of service, to be part of her healing journey.

Step 18: We thank Source and all the higher frequency beings who took part in this session. This was a collective effort, and we were the transmitter of their energy.

Step 19: We drink another glass of water and replenish our bodies after transmitting this divine high frequency. Our physical bodies need to hydrate after a session. This is also the time to offer water to the animal as well. Their bodies and ours need water to conduct the energy with more ease. The energy continues to flow internally in their bodies for several days after the session has been completed.

Step 20: We write down any messages we may have received during this session. I recommend always having a journal in our healing session space so we can easily jot down messages immediately after completion of the session. It is common to receive messages when we are in this space of deep connection. We may be able then to share them with the person who asked us to help their beloved animal companion.

I typically do sessions in the evening so that I can rest after. The sessions are not draining nor damaging but the bodies did something that required a very high surge of unconditional love frequency all at once, and it is best to give it time to recalibrate before moving on to our daily routine. We each have a body that has different needs. It is wise to take a couple of hours to rest after a session.

We may feel a little winded, perhaps we feel we need to ground ourselves better, perhaps we are quite invigorated. Each of us will respond differently after a session; therefore, it is wise to listen to our bodies before engaging in the next physical activity.

ADDITIONAL GUIDANCE FOR THE ENERGY HEALING SESSION

We always hold the highest unconditional love frequency possible when working with any animals. This means no pity, sorrow, grief, fear, anxiety, sadness, or anger should be present during the session. If we are feeling anything other than peace in our hearts, let's pay very close attention to the three preliminary steps listed in my method of healing. The last thing we want is to project these low frequencies to the animal and exacerbate the ailment they suffer from.

Let's adjust the time we send unconditional love frequency to our animal based on the need or intention of the moment. It does not have to be a specific set amount of time like sixty minutes or even thirty minutes. We do this transmission for the amount that feels right. The animal will also indicate to us when she has had enough and will walk away. We can always come back the following day and do another part of the session. I do this when my body is tired, jet-lagged, or other.

Let's always listen to our bodies!

The outcome we desire when sending unconditional love frequency is that we are fully present, and we are in our highest state of vibration possible. If that requires extra rest before proceeding, we need to take the rest. This is in the best interest of the beloved animal we intend to provide service to.

If doing the session in person, the animal may choose to have us place our hands on them. They will nudge us or quite literally come in contact with us. We can then feel free to touch the animals anytime they request it. It is their choice, and they can certainly receive unconditional love frequency from our hearts and from our hands simultaneously. Unconditional love frequency is received by physical contact but also by the frequency we emit. Both work and both are well received. The choice of which to select for any given session lies within the animal, not us.

Let's always allow the animal to have the choice of leaving the room or the space where the energy healing is taking place. A few minutes may be sufficient, in which case, the animal companion

PART 7: BATHE ANIMAL COMPANIONS WITH THE FREQUENCY OF LOVE

should always have the freedom to walk away. Let's remember, we offer the healing, but it is the animal who chooses how much to receive or if to receive it at all. We respect the animal's sovereignty.

If we have been attuned to Reiki and would like to practice the symbols, mudras, or affirmations while doing the unconditional love frequency session, we can certainly do so. One modality of healing does not negate the other, it only enhances it. It is beneficial to use Reiki symbols although not required for the healing to be successful.

It is our choice to use other chakras to also send unconditional love frequency to the animal companion. I focus on the heart chakra exclusively because this is the antenna that receives higher frequencies. However, it is not the only power center in the body we can use to transmit energy.

We can certainly change it up and find what chakra or combination of chakras feel more natural to us when doing this practice. With time, we will know. Each animal is different. Each session is different. Each day we may be in a different space. All these factors will determine what will feel right in each session. We have the freedom to adjust accordingly.

Projecting unconditional love frequency and bathing the animal in it can also be amplified and expanded as desired. Let's say we are working at the Humane Society, and we want to bring healing to multiple animals at once. We can expand our field to reach them all. I recommend focusing on one at a time for the most powerful results, but working on several animals at once is also possible and in certain cases such as this, very much recommended for the benefit of all the animals in need of healing.

There is no need to practice unconditional love frequency healing with the animal daily. In fact, I recommend allowing time for integration to occur before doing the next session. Depending on the health of the animal, this could be a week or it could be a month. It is important to give the animal's body time to adjust to the higher frequencies that were received. We need to allow them enough time to recalibrate their bodies before adding on more. More is not necessarily better. The quality of our intentionality over the frequency of the sessions is my personal recommendation.

If we feel guided to work on a specific part of the body and focus all the unconditional love frequency and attention to that part, by all means, we can certainly do so. This is most likely the animal telling us where the energy is needed most. We will then do as requested.

As we work with energy, we may begin to relate certain colors with certain frequencies. We follow our hearts and choose the color that speaks to us in that specific moment. There is a reason. Energy has its nuances and as we practice, we learn to trust what our inner guidance tells us. Colors are the visual representation of frequencies. Multiple frequencies, multiple colors. We can feel free to experiment.

One session I may work on an animal visualizing a combination of golden, white, rainbow energy. Another day I may choose a vibrant green energy only. As mentioned before, each animal is different, each session is different. We can tailor to their needs and that means different colors, different duration, and different adjustments to be in their service.

On certain occasions I use an animal anatomy chart to work on one organ at a time. This is recommended if we want to specifically locate the source of the health problem. We can then scan each organ individually. By using this chart, we will be able to identify the specific organ that is having the energy imbalance. This is the area to which we will focus our energy healing.

On other occasions, I work on the chakras of the animal by using a chakra chart of the animal species I am working on. This helps me be very intentional in realigning the animal's power centers equally.

Chakras are located in slightly different places depending on the animal species.

Working with these different approaches depending on the situation will allow us to fine-tune the practice to create the best experience for the animal.

Benefits of regular sessions with our beloved animal companions include: a calmer personality, happier animal, better physical health, better quality of life, and longevity. Issues such as anxiety, stress, and reactivity are significantly reduced. Pain, inflammation, and digestive disorders can be reduced as well. In the end, all these benefits lead to a higher quality of life and the ability to live longer. For those of us who have animal companions at home, knowing we can give them the gift of a better or longer life is priceless. It is all about harnessing the superpower we have in our hearts and practicing holding that frequency of unconditional love for several minutes every day.

I invite us all to practice love, at the same time each day, to establish a habit in our daily routine. We will be amazed at what changes we get to witness. The more changes we see, the more we will be motivated to stick to our daily practice. It is a symbiotic relationship where we bring these benefits to our beloved animal companions and in return, our animals give us more quality time with them.

Here is an example of what practicing this technique can do for the beautiful animals in our life. What are we waiting for? I promise, our beloved animals will be so very grateful!

KITTY WITH STOMACH SENSITIVITY

I received a call from a yoga instructor whose cat Shiva was having stomach issues. I have been working on Shiva for a while, and because they live nearby, I have worked with her in person each time.

Each time the kitty responds very well to the energy healing. She stretches her body and takes it all in. She does not walk or move away. She stays in the same location near me and shows signs of relaxation and complete surrender to the process. It is a joy to see her enjoy the session in such a way.

Time after time, her stomach issues return. Different natural remedies and a change of diet are recommended but her problems return months later.

One day I connected with Shiva to inquire about where this sensitivity is originating from that diet has not been able to resolve. She showed me an image of her cat mother who looked malnourished, not in great health. She was not sick but fragile and vulnerable. As Shiva was feeding from her mother, she was unable to receive critical nutrients that would allow her to develop a strong immune system and a strong microbiome. This image alone explained quite clearly why her stomach sensitivity was a recurring pattern.

I relayed the information to her human companion so she would be able to take all needed measures to work on fortifying and strengthening her immune system. Had I not connected with Shiva, I would have never known the root of her problems.

The good news is, knowing this allows Shiva's mom to work with the vet to find viable options to improve her immunity. An informed cat mother means an empowered caretaker.

WHAT I LEARNED FROM THIS STORY

It is very important to always come with a very open mind to every session. The challenges animals experience may originate with their parents. Many things are transmitted from animal parents to their babies.

I fully believe that knowledge empowers us to make better choices and have better awareness, which means having a better chance at a

PART 7: BATHE ANIMAL COMPANIONS WITH THE FREQUENCY OF LOVE

smoother journey in this life. What if we can do the same for our beloved animal companions?

I hope this book has helped us all initiate the process of unlearning those patterns that have stopped us from maximizing our full divine potential.

I hope my animal practice gives us all the tools to share the frequency of love with all creatures on Earth, starting with our beloved animal companions in our own homes.

I hope we develop a beautiful connection with Source to thrive in life like we never have before.

I hope we know happiness is possible and it starts with shifting perspectives every moment of our life. When we harness happiness, we reconnect with our superpower.

May this book take us all to places we never thought we would go in life starting right now! I invite us all to try one or two of the steps in my practice and integrate them into our lives for a full year. Let's see the changes. Let's see for ourselves how different we feel. If we are building inner peace, perhaps let's try a couple of more techniques. The most transformational changes in life are the addition of those small steps we take each day.

Big changes do not happen overnight. The power of microchanges is deeply life altering. I invite us all to take that small first step, then the next, and the next. I speak from experience when I say, this practice will be one of the best investments in our happiness. It changed me. I know each and every one of us can change too.

I would like to conclude with this poem I wrote during the pandemic. For those moments when happiness feels a little harder to reach, may this poem restore the hope needed to keep creating happiness in our hearts and sharing it with the world.

Hope

May I be peace in the middle of the storm.
May I shine bright in times of darkness.
May I be hope in times of despair.
May I stand strong to uplift the fallen.
May I open the hearts of those who are shut down.
May I be neutral in front of conflict.
May I bring comfort to those who have given up.
May I be a loving shoulder to those who need to cry.
May I bring a new perspective when all seems lost.
May I be a bouquet of colorful flowers when all seems black.
May I be the one to lean on for those who feel alone.
May I be the love needed by those who suffer.
May I be the strength for those who can't go any further.
May I open the eyes of those blinded by fear.
May I be the reminder that there is always a better tomorrow.
May I be the ocean that washes away sorrows.
May I be the gentle breeze that kisses everyone's face.
May I be the ray of sunshine that warms everyone's heart.
May I be the earth beneath everyone's feet that supports and holds us all strong.
May I be the drops of rain that clear away all doubt.
May I be unconditional love emanating from the perfume of a rose.
May I bring laughter to those falling prey to

depression.

May I help everyone see the world through the eyes of a child, to always be amazed by the beauty hidden around every corner.

May I be the reminder that we ALL are in this together, and nobody is alone.

May I be at all times more than my story, so everyone remembers they are not their story either.

—Stephanie

RESOURCES

Breath of Gold Breathwork https://www.breathofgold.com/

High Functioning by Psychiatrist Dr. Judith Joseph

Masaru Emoto "Water Crystals" https://masaruemoto.net/en/science-of-messages-from-water/

The Emotion Code by Bradley Nelson.

The New Earth by Eckhart Tolle

Transcending the Levels of Consciousness: The Stairway to Enlightenment by Sir Dr. David R. Hawkins

Underground Waters by Glenn Broughton

What the Bleep Do We Know? Movie released in 2004.

Your Soul's Plan by Robert Schwartz

STEPHANIE STEPHAN

Stephanie is an animal lover who listens and observes from the heart. She has developed a unique blend of communication, intuition, and healing that has the potential to create a deeper bond between you and your animal companion, fostering a sense of harmony that resonates on all levels: emotional, physical, energetic and spiritual. She has learned how these divine sentient beings are capable of opening the door to infinite wisdom and unconditional love. When we open our hearts to them, they can teach us life mysteries that lead to having a more joyful life. They are the key to unlock our superpower that resides within.

To learn more about her offerings, you are invited to visit her at: www.unconditional-love-frequency-with-stephanie-stephan.com/

For more great books from Peak View Press
Visit Books.GracePointPublishing.com

If you enjoyed reading *The Path to Unconditional Love* and purchased it through an online retailer, please return to the site and write a review to help others find the book.

www.ingramcontent.com/pod-product-compliance
Lightning Source LLC
Chambersburg PA
CBHW050550160426
43199CB00015B/2606